The Moon Manual

By Quinn K. Dyer & Morgan V. Fay

Disclaimer:

This book does not replace the advice of a medical professional. We do not accept responsibility for the use or misuse of any information found in this book. All information provided is for entertainment purposes only and the outcome of any ritual or spell cannot be guaranteed.

TABLE OF CONTENTS:

INTRODUCTION

The gentle influence of the moon's cycles affects our magick as much as they affect the tides.

Our magickal workings can be planned according to these lunar cycles, and in this book, we outline how the zodiac signs and the phases of the moon work in tandem to affect our magick, as well as how various herbs & crystals mesh with those changing energies. Many witches are familiar with the flow of the waning & waxing phases of the moon, and how they affect spellwork, but less so with how the signs of the zodiac can influence the moon.

If you aren't familiar with those waxing & waning cycles and how to utilize them for magickal work, understanding their patterns is really quite simple.

In general, the new moon corresponds to new beginnings & setting intentions for the upcoming cycle. The waxing phases promote growth, positive magick, and drawing energy to us, while the waning phases push away and the energies are destructive in nature. The energies of the waxing moon peak just before the full moon, and the energies of the waning moon peak just before the dark moon. And the full moon can be

utilized for a myriad of magickal purposes. It has the
strongest lunar energy of the moon's cycle, but as you will
see, the zodiac can heavily influence those lunar energies.

The moon spends about 2.5 days in each zodiac sign as she
travels through her 28 days cycle. Certain patterns emerge &
are fairly constant during this cycle.

For example, during a new moon, both the sun & the moon
reside in the same sign. Just as, during a full moon, the sun
resides in the sign opposite the moon's.

The waxing & waning phases also follow patterns with a zodiac
sign only seeing the waxing phases during one half of the
year and the waning during the other half. That being said, a
crescent or gibbous moon can occur in the same sign multiple
times during the year; sometimes within just a few months of
each other or in consecutive months.

Keep an eye out for other cycles the moon goes through as
well, such as blue moons, black moons & eclipses. A blue moon
is the second full moon in a single calendar month, and this
auspicious moon amplifies luck, growth & divination magick.
Contrarily, a black moon refers to a second new moon in one
calendar month. It is a perfect period for change. Under this
powerful moon, take the first steps in turning an area of
your life around.

Eclipses are also extremely powerful celestial events with
somewhat chaotic energy. Lunar eclipses favor working with
the sun & solar magick, as the sun blocks the moon's light.
Conversely, solar eclipses favor moon-related magick, as the
moon blocks the sun.

Another important astrological event to take note of is the

'void-of-course' moon. The 'void-of-course' moon is the period when the moon is transitioning between zodiac signs. It begins after the moon has had her last major interaction with the planets, and ends when the moon moves into the next sign. In order to know when this happens & for how long, it is necessary to consult an astrological chart, and there are many available online!

We are firm believers that while your intention powers your spellwork, our magickal works still rely heavily on not only what tools you have available, but also the astrological timing we choose to perform them.

While there are recipes & directions for spellwork within this book, the idea behind it is to give you the tools to write & formulate your own spells based on those lunar correspondences & cycles, rather than provide specific rituals. It is important to personalize your craft!

♈ Aries Magick

RULING PLANET:
Mars ♂

SPELLS FOR:
self-improvement
protection
strength
healing
leadership

FIRE MAGICK: △
Under a fire sign, like Aries, the moon vibes with magick involving fire, incense & candles.

Fire's elemental direction is south.

The element of fire is also associated with. wands or ceremonial blades.

CRYSTALS:
garnet, diamond, carnelian, red jasper, bloodstone & ruby

TAROT:
the Emperor
king of pentacles
queen of wands
2,3,4 of wands

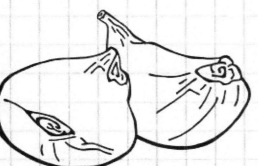

HERBS:
garlic, clove, honeysuckle, nettles, hops, yarrow, thyme, basil & sage

Magick for the Aries New Moon

The Aries new moon occurs with the sun also in Aries, around the end of March or beginning of April — just around the spring equinox, at least in the Northern Hemisphere. In the Southern half of the globe, it is the fall equinox instead!

The new moon is when the moon is caught between the sun & the earth and is no longer visible. When the moon is truly dark in the sky, it is best to refrain from major spellwork.

It is a much better time to prepare for the upcoming lunar cycle. Instead, try some spellwork or activities to aid in introspection & reflection, including self-growth, recharging, or renewal. Under active Aries, try yoga or going for a walk!

Of course, this is also a great time to set intentions and goals for the future. Burn a bay leaf or two with what you wish to accomplish during the upcoming lunar cycle written upon it. Use a second leaf if you run out of space!

And while the new moon is a great time for starting fresh,

don't expect Aries to give you lasting results; things started under Aries lack staying power. Spells can be short-lived and Aries' energies can cause impatience, impulsiveness & carelessness to stand in the way of your spellwork as well.

Just don't try to restraint Aries' energy with too much thinking! This is a sign of action & energy — don't fight it!

For fire signs, like Aries, magick involving fire, incense, or candles is supercharged. Harness the double dose of fiery Aries energy with some extra potent candle magick. Save ashes from your incense, smudging, or smoking to mix with salt for casting a circle.

Or carve an intention into a candle & let it burn. A candle is a beautiful & powerful tool that harnesses & represents the four elements — fire for the flame, air to stoke it, water for the melted wax, and earth for the solid wax.

Considering that both the moon & sun in Aries, give to respect this fire sign by snuffing your candles rather than blowing them out — an act that puts air above fire. Save blowing out your candles for when the celestial bodies are in an air sign.

The colors of your candles can be tailored to your spells as well, but if you're ever in doubt a white candle can be safely used to replace any color candle. And using multiple different colored candles in one spell can also power up your results. There are even more possibilities when you consider candles can also come in a variety of shapes that can be coordinated to your intent as well!

Try burning a black candle on your altar next to a candle colored to match your spell's intents before lighting it. The black candle will reverse any negative energy surrounding your intention and clears the path for smooth casting.

This elemental energy is best put to use when you are seeking rapid results from your spellwork, but not long-lasting ones. Fast & unpredictable, remember that fire can eat up everything in its path in an instant!

Healing & protection spells are good in Aries. A few medicinal herbs with protective qualities that sync well with Aries include yarrow, sage, nettles, and especially garlic!

Eggshells are known for their protective energies. Wash & save your eggshells after cooking, and when dry, grind them down with a mortar & pestle or food processor. The powder can be used to cast circles or line thresholds to ward away bad energy. If you don't eat eggs, you can always ask your friends & family for scraps. Eggshells found in nature are wonderful gifts & perfect for spellwork. Just always be sure that you are washing your shells thoroughly!

Magick for the Aries Waxing Crescent Moon

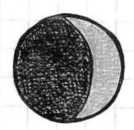

The Aries waxing crescent moon occurs from October to April, which means the sun can reside in Libra, Scorpio, Sagittarius, Capricorn, Aquarius, Pisces, Aries, or Taurus during this time. Tailor your spells to fit the energies of both.

For example, both Aries & Pisces aid us in pursuing our creative dreams. Call down creativity & let your inspiration swell with the moon. This phase is perfect for pulling our desires towards us.

Both the Aries moon & the waxing crescent phase aid in inspiring passion in life, love & at work. Anoint a red candle — for passion — with thyme oil — for courage. Carve a rune or an intention into it, then let it burn to gather strength & courage to chase your passions. Candle magick is supercharged under fiery Aries.

In fact, Aries' firey energy can leave us basking in spontaneity & initiative to get things done. Yet, impatience causes us to fall out of alignment with the universe — don't let Aries' energies let you do so! It can be the downfall of spellwork! Trust in yourself & in your magick to succeed!

The protective herb, garlic has strong associations with the zodiac sign Aries. And aligning your protection spells with an Aries moon is a great idea; as Aries is a sign that is particularly good for protective spellwork.

Try some potent kitchen magic yourself with this protection spell for Roasted Garlic:

I. Preheat oven to 400 degrees.
2. Cut the top off a head of garlic, so all the cloves are exposed.
3. Place in a ceramic roasting pan, or on tin foil on a cooking sheet.
4. Drizzle liberally with olive oil, and state your intention aloud: that this meal should impart protection to all those who partake.
5. (For a spell with an extra kick try a herbal infusion in your oil.)
6. Place the lid on your roasting pan or wrap the head loosely in tinfoil — it should be able to breathe.
7. Cook for 30-40 minutes or until the garlic is tender.

Serve with bread and olive oil.

Magick for the Aries First Quarter Moon

The Aries first quarter moon can occur from October to April. This means that at this time the sun can be in Libra, Scorpio, Sagittarius, Capricorn, Aquarius, Pisces, Aries, or Taurus, and the energies of both those signs should be considered in spellwork as well.

Aries is one of the best signs for casting protection spells, but with the sun in sensitive Pisces those efforts may flounder. However, if the sun resides under another sign, cast away! Ward your doors with bundles of herbs or an herbal wash; sage & nettles work well with Aries' vibes. Or soak in a bath with an infusion of basil, chamomile, or sage.

Healing & medicinal work is good in Aries as well as Libra or Pisces. Add an extra oomph to herbal salves, tinctures & syrups by brewing them at this time. Aries & garlic both lend themselves to speedy healing.

Make a simple remedy for a sore throat to keep on hand with honey & garlic. Fill a jar with peeled garlic cloves & cover them with honey. Let the mixture sit for a few days until the honey tastes strongly of garlic, while the waxing moon's energies aid in drawing out the medicinal properties. To use, take a teaspoon of honey to soothe a sore throat or eat an entire clove to ingest those amazing anti-inflammatory & immune-boosting properties.

Certain types of spells also vibe well with particular times of the day. For example, healing spells work well with dawn & the early morning!

During the quarter moon, it is a good time to take action and to take steps towards manifesting what you started at the last new moon. And boy, is Aries a sign of action. When the moon is in Aries, we can feel more impulsive & self-confident. This can help! Don't get bogged down thinking; just do the thing!

Getting your headspace right can make all the difference for tackling big, intimidating projects. Work with Aries' energy by going for a walk beforehand. Find something grounding in nature, like a stone or a pinecone, and – so long as it is safe to do so – bring it home and place it on your altar.

Scented candles also work wonders for setting a mood by combining candle & color magick with aromas. Jasmine boosts confidence , while tangerine is energizing and sparks child-like playfulness.

For fire signs, like Aries, magick involving fire is intensified. Fire's energy is creative; the light of even a few candles can be inspiring.

Magick for the Aries Waxing Gibbous Moon

The Aries waxing gibbous moon occurs from October to April. During this time the sun can reside in Libra, Scorpio, Sagittarius, Capricorn, Aquarius, Pisces, Aries, or Taurus.

The waxing phases are perfect for constructive magick of all sorts; spells for magick that pulls our desires towards us. During the waxing gibbous phase, there is little time to harness that energy before the full moon.

The waxing gibbous in particular helps spells meant to renew & restore strength. Aries's energy can put a stop to feeling burnt out. Just take some time for self-care. After all, Aries is selfish. Spells should focus on oneself, such as those for self-improvement.

Aries also helps us chase our passions; write your desires on sage leaves to burn & release into the universe. Incorporate candles, to amp up Aries' creative fiery energies, by ringing them around yourself as you cast. And with the sun in Pisces, Aquarius, or Sagittarius, those creative vibes are amplified.

Just keep in mind that Aries' energy lacks staying power.
Spells cast under an Aries moon tend to be short-lived.

Even under energetic Aries, dealing with negative people can
be draining, so protect yourself! Black tourmaline in
particular is a champion against toxic energies. Carry the
stone in your pocket to fight negativity — both internal &
external.

Or stuff a sachet to carry with protective herbs like
rosemary or sage, and other protective crystals like amber,
bloodstone, or obsidian. Be sure to put in a few cloves of
garlic too! They just work so well with Aries' energy!

A few cloves of chopped garlic can also be added into a mix
for protection circles; try with sea salt and protection
herbs before casting.

Or light a black candle — a color of security, strength &
protection — for yourself or a loved one. To direct your
intent etch their name or initials into the candle wax. Just
remember to always be respectful when performing magick that
involves others.

Healing work is also good under Aries.

Magick for the Aries Full Moon

The Aries full moon occurs when the sun is in Libra. During the full moon, the earth is caught directly between the sun & the moon. This gives us the most powerful lunar energy in the moon's cycle. Emotions, intuition & creativity are all heightened at this time.

As the Libra season spans from September to October, this means the Aries full moon only occurs during one of these two months. If it is September then the moon is the Harvest Moon, but in October it would be the Hunter's Moon.

Dreamwork & divination come naturally at the full moon, but in Aries, this work is best left alone.

It is, however, an excellent time to bless blades. Light a candle in the sight of the full moon and bless your ritual blades by sliding them through the flame. Blades, runes, tarot cards, water, crystals & more can all be charged in the moonlight as well!

Coffee vibes well with Aries. Draw sigils for courage,

strength, or protection in your morning brew and sip. It's a great power boost to nearly any spell and a bit of simple magick for a low-energy day!

Libra helps Aries to be less self-absorbed, making healing work excellent under the Aries full moon. It's a perfect time for sewing & stuffing a healing poppet. Or brewing herbal salves, tinctures & syrups.

With the sun in Libra, try working with elderberries; their energies pair well. Elderberry syrup is easy to make if you have access to fresh berries. Remember homemade remedies are no replacement for actual medical care! Here is the recipe:

- 2 ounces of cooked berries (see below)
- I cup of honey
- 2 cups of water
- Saucepan and spoon

1. Combine cooked berries and water in a saucepan over a low heat. Bring to simmer and reduce water by half. (Berries can be easily cooked by boiling in water, then reducing to a simmer & cooking berries for about 20 minutes or until they are soft.)
2. Strain plant matter through cheesecloth and return liquid to the saucepan.
3. Add honey, heat to II5°F & mix until honey is dissolved. Let cool.
4. Store in the refrigerator.

Take no more than I tablespoon 3x a day for adults; kids I teaspoon.

It's important to never, ever eat raw berries. They are toxic raw and can cause vomiting and a whole mess of other digestive issues. So just don't!

You can also sync up your spellwork to the time of day as well. Healing energies are strongest at dawn, while spells for courage & strength are better done at noon.

While Mars, Aries' ruling planet, is the planet of aggression, it can also be used to release frustration & anger. Take a fresh egg or an old, empty soda can outside — wear sturdy shoes! Breathe & visualize the cause of your anger. Then, crush the egg or soda can under your shoe — really stomp on it! If possible, scream while you stomp to really get that frustration out. A shower or smoke cleanse is a great follow-up to cleanse your energy, and of course, remember to clean up the can or your shoe!

Aries' enthusiastic energy can cause us to be impulsive & carefree, maybe even careless, so take care with your spellwork. That reckless energy can also be somewhat short-lived. Spells started under Aries will tend to not be long lasting, so plan accordingly.

You can use the other elements to help balance out another. Employ water & earth into your spellwork to soothe & slow the burn of fire.

Magick for the Aries Waning Gibbous Moon

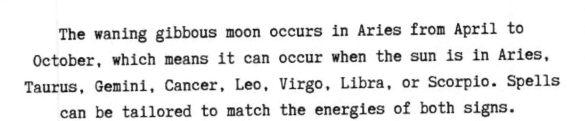

The waning gibbous moon occurs in Aries from April to October, which means it can occur when the sun is in Aries, Taurus, Gemini, Cancer, Leo, Virgo, Libra, or Scorpio. Spells can be tailored to match the energies of both signs.

For example, Cancer & Aries both vibe with protection magick, while Leo & Aries can power spells for courage, self-confidence, or strength.

Don't forget to take the time of year into account too. The waning Aries moon can occur more than once from spring to fall, meaning there are plenty of fresh flowers & herbs to use as spell ingredients, offerings & altar decor.

The waning moon pushes away what we do not want and is great for magick that repels, banishes & destroys.
You can use that energy to banish self-doubt as the energies after a full moon aid in introspection.

Bless a blade & use it to metaphorically chop that self-doubt down. Or take an herbal bath with sunflowers, basil, chamomile, St. John's wort, or lemon balm. Let all the bad juju get washed down the drain. You can supercharge your spell with firepower & ring the tub with as many candles as you safely can. Or just a few!

Aries is a sign of action & energy, but for the few days after the full moon, energies can feel sapped & slow as the moon recedes. So take it easy! Rest is just as important as action!

The waning gibbous is a great phase for breaking bad habits & Aries is great for spells that focus on yourself. Just be careful what you start as the effects of spells can be short-lived when the moon is in Aries. So try spellwork that requires rapid results, rather than long-term ones.

With the moon in Aries, impatience, impulsiveness & carelessness can also stand in the way of your spellwork.

The waning moon is also a great time to cleanse any new candle, crystal, or tools of any negative vibes they might have picked up before you. Many people with many energies might have handled a candle before you purchased it. Under fiery Aries, incense cleansing is especially potent — and in the spirit of Aries, take no time at all!

Simply light your incense and pass your items through the wisps of smoke. Visualize any clinging energy being wiped away by the fragrant smoke trails. Let your incense burn out on its own — as long as it's safe & monitored. Never go to sleep with incense burning!

Magick for the Aries Last Quarter Moon

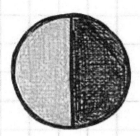

The Aries last quarter moon occurs from April to October, which means it can occur when the sun is in Aries, Taurus, Gemini, Cancer, Leo, Virgo, Libra, or Scorpio.

Your spellwork can use the energies of both the sun & the moon. For example, medicinal work is strong under Aries as well as Gemini. Use the waning moon to banish illness. After all, the waning phases are most conducive to magick that repels, banishes, or destroys.

Aries is a sign of action; try incorporating dance & movement into your spellwork or walking out your circle as you cast to take advantage of how Aries' energy flows through us.

The Aries last quarter moon is good for dealing with transitions & temptations. When the moon resides under self-interested Aries, spells should focus on yourself. Break & banish bad habits; the waning moon is excellent for this. Write down bad habits & bind with sage, thyme & black thread. Burn the entire bundle.

For fire signs, magick involving fire is potent. Try blessing a blade and use it to carve a candle. Burn incense and save the ashes to mix with salt to use for protection circles. You can also try casting your protection circle with a ring of candles. Don't ever be afraid to personalize a spell! Follow your intuition!

Just remember that things started under Aries lack staying power. Results from spells will be short-lived. Just like fire, it can be unpredictable & fast-moving, but it is a perfect time to cast if you are looking for fast results!

With all that extra energy that Aries brings, it is a perfect time for short-term projects & crafts you've wanted to try. Things that can be completed in a day will satisfy Aries's impatience.

Out of ideas? Try making your own candles for future spellwork — and to keep those hands busy! Here's a recipe for at-home scented soy candles:

I. Melt 8oz of soy wax over medium-low heat.
2. Add 40-80 drops of essential oils of your choice to the melted wax.
3. Anchor your wick to the bottom of a jar with a dab of wax, then secure the top by taping the other end to a pen or chopstick resting across the top of the jar.
4. Pour in wax and let set.

Optionally, dried herbs, colorants, or even fire-safe crystals can be added into the wax to empower specific intentions.

Magick for the Aries Waning Crescent Moon

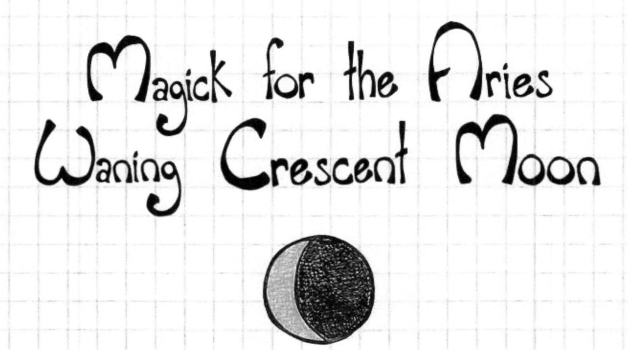

The waning crescent in Aries can occur from April to October, so at this time the sun can be in Aries, Taurus, Gemini, Cancer, Leo, Virgo, Libra, or Scorpio.

Spellwork can be tailored to match the energies of both these signs. Harness the protective energies of Cancer & Aries with a circle of garlic & salt around your home. Or amp up your spellwork with fire; burn dried nettles & sage — they work well with Aries' protective vibes. Use it to banish bad energy & protect your home.

In an apartment or other small space? Anoint the four farthest corners of your home with protective oils like peppermint or sage, or burn four black candles there — black is the color of protection & security.

The waning crescent is an immensely powerful time for casting banishing spells & casting out anything you no longer want in your life. This close to the dark moon is when these energies are at their strongest. Under Aries, let self-doubt or illness wane away with the moon.

Healing & medicinal work is especially good with Aries'
energy, as well as Gemini; banish illness with a bit of
kitchen witchery. Brew up a simple restorative soup stock
with medicinal herbs:

I. Chop an onion and several pieces of celery and carrots
   into large pieces.
2. Add all veggies to a large soup pot with leftover chicken
   or turkey carcass & whole nettles.
3. Flavor to taste with rosemary, bay leaves, garlic, thyme,
   salt & pepper.
4. Bring to a boil and then let simmer for 2 hours. Stir
   occasionally, always counterclockwise, to banish, while
   whispering your intent.
5. Strain out solid matter and freeze the liquid.

This stock can be saved for several months and used to cook
many dishes with & imbue them with healing energy.

Remember that things started under Aries are often short-
lived. Spells are only powerful for a short while — so plan
for them to work thus.

And although they can be overcome, Aries' energies can cause
impatience, carelessness, or impulsiveness to stand in the
way of success with spellwork.

Taurus Magick

RULING PLANET: ♀
Venus

SPELLS FOR:
money & prosperity
love & relationships
creativity
luck
trust

EARTH MAGICK: ▽

When the moon is in an earth sign, like Taurus, magick involving crystals, stones, salt, dirt, or roots is powerful.

Earth's elemental direction is north.

The element of earth is also associated with pentacles & besoms.

CRYSTALS:
amber, aventurine, emerald, jade, malachite & turquoise

HERBS:

sage, daisy, thyme, mint, goldenseal, parsley, rosemary, mugwort, rose, nettles & catnip

TAROT:

the Hierophant
king of pentacles
knight of swords
5,6,7 of pentacles

Magick for the Taurus New Moon

The new, or dark, moon in Taurus occurs with the sun also in Taurus, in late April or early May. Which, in the Northern Hemisphere, places it around Beltane. Aptly, this is the most fertile moon of the year and one of the best times to cast spellwork for abundance, prosperity, fertility, luck, or money-drawing.

The new moon is also when you should set intentions for the upcoming lunar cycle. Visualize your goals and figure out what you need to manifest them.

Fertile Taurus helps us move beyond providing for our basic needs; to grow and blossom and create abundance. Spells begun in Taurus have long-lasting results and can be next to impossible to stop. In fact, the earthy energies of Taurus are best put to use for spells that are meant to grow & gather strength slowly. The element grants the endurance & stamina necessary for long-term success.

Write long-term goals on a scrap of paper or a bay leaf & bury them under the dark moon in your garden or under a potted plant — an earthly place of growth. Taurus also amps up earth magick.

You can also try tapping into those earthen energies by molding your intentions into clay. It's a wonderful material for working magick. It's possible to create runes, poppets, charms, offering dishes, candle holders, cups, and more.

Clay can be kept soft to be easily reworked or disposed of — just make sure you cleanse it before reusing it! Or clay can be baked and made hard to make your intent more permanent.

Spellwork for money-drawing & luck is also in sync with the Taurus new moon's energies. Bergamot & mint, which help attract wealth can be put to use. Brew up a mint julep or bergamot tea & sip. A drizzle of moon water into your brew can help the potion pack an extra punch!

As symbols of spring, fresh daisies can be used as an altar decoration this time of year. When worn, the flower brings luck & love. They can be incorporated into rituals & used as offerings as well!

The moon's cleansing energy thrives in Taurus too. Treat yourself to a hot bath with sage & rosemary. Infuse hot water with herbs or use an herbal bath bomb! Let yourself enjoy wine, chocolates, or a good book while you soak. Taurus and Venus, the sign's ruling planet, love luxury.

Cooking is another way to indulge both Taurus & Venus's sensual natures. Shortbread is a delicious treat that can be made with pressed herbs to imbue the cookies with the herb's properties. Here is an easy recipe:

• 2 cups of flour

- I cup of sugar
- ½ teaspoon salt
- I cup room temperature, unsalted butter
- A few bunches of fresh herbs

I. Preheat oven to 325°F.
2. Combine all ingredients with a mixer. Then, knead by hand until the dough no longer crumbles.
3. Chill for I5 minutes, then roll out the dough with a rolling pin to roughly ½ inch thickness.
4. Cut out your cookies with a cookie cutter & gently press your foliage into each cookie. A single leaf or petal will work well in some cases, but some flowerheads are small enough to be completely used. Cookies can be covered with wax paper & lightly rolled again with a rolling pin to further press the herbs into the dough.
5. Bake for I8-22 minutes. The bottoms will just be turning golden, and the cookie may look soft before cooling.

It can be fun to experiment with herbal correspondences & these cookies. There are many herbs that can be used, including rosemary, borage, lavender, parsley, sage, thyme, mugwort & more! The choice is up to you!

Any spells pertaining to trust, loyalty, friendship, bonding, and harmony in relationships are also great under the double Taurean energy. Love spells too, but only for already established, long-term relationships — nothing manipulative if you can help it!

The double Taurean energy can even be put to work in joint spellcasting. Set intentions with a partner — platonic or romantic.

Magick for the Taurus Waxing Crescent Moon

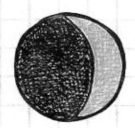

The waxing crescent moon in Taurus occurs from November to May. This means that at this time the sun can be in either Taurus, Gemini, Cancer, Leo, Virgo, Libra, Scorpio, or Sagittarius.

Money, prosperity & fertility spells are also great to cast under both Taurus & Virgo. Taurus helps us grow and create abundance, especially during a waxing moon, and Taurus tends to give us long-lasting results.

A pinecone with the seeds still inside can be kept as a charm for fertility & prosperity. However, do not pull one from a tree yourself; it still belongs to the tree & will not have value in your spellwork.

Lodestones, or natural magnets, aid in drawing things towards us, and put Taurus's earthy energies to good use. Anoint a lodestone with oil & herbs for money-drawing. Then, add the lodestone to a dish with change to attract more cash. Keep adding coins to the dish as the moon waxes.

Mint, thyme & sage are all great money-drawing herbs to use under Taurus. Get your hands dirty and plant a penny under one of these herbs to help your funds grow.

Relish the dirt under your nails, as the Taurus moon amps up earth magick, and this can be doubly powerful when the sun is also in an earth sign, like Taurus or Virgo. You can draw sigils with salt, carve a charm from a sturdy root, or bury a crystal to charge while the moon waxes.

Grab a bath bomb or add some bubbles & enjoy; Taurus loves the luxurious. Take a hot herbal soak. There's nothing more Tauran than low-effort magick.

Any & all non-manipulative bonding magic or any love spells pertaining to trust, loyalty & harmony in relationships can be cast during a Taurus moon. The waxing moon is particularly good for drawing these energies out.

Conjure up some love by infusing lavender, marjoram & catnip into honey. Let it soak in the moonlight & wax with the moon. Use the entire waxing cycle. At the next full moon, take a taste & don't forget to lick your fingers clean!

No significant other? Use the bonding capabilities of the Taurus moon to grow friendship or self-love.

If you are hoping to draw new people into your life, pull out your tarot deck & choose a card that depicts the type of person you would like to see in your life – platonic or romantic. Then place the card on your altar for the duration of the waxing cycle & open your mind. It is important not to focus on a specific person, only the qualities.

Magick for the Taurus First Quarter Moon

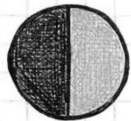

The first quarter moon in Taurus can occur from November to May, and at this time the sun can reside in Taurus, Gemini, Cancer, Leo, Virgo, Libra, Scorpio, or Sagittarius.

The waxing moon is for growth & pulling our desires towards us. These energies are at their peak during the quarter moon, and the moon's energy is particularly potent in Taurus; it is a good time to take action.

Fertile Taurus helps us to create abundance & gives us the tools to achieve material success. It's a good time to plant the seeds of success, both literal & figurative. Spells for money & prosperity are extremely potent, especially during a waxing moon.

Add money-drawing herbs to a sachet or stuff them into a poppet with a snippet of your hair, to represent yourself. Dress the doll in green & gold to help attract prosperity and keep it on your altar while the moon waxes. Sage, rosemary & thyme can help attract cash and are also quite delicious.

Taurus loves the pleasures of the material world, so try cooking up some magick in the kitchen.

Bread — a staple to many witches — is especially powerful in earth signs, and the breaking of bread is always best done with friends, family & loved ones. Combine these money-drawing herbs and bread into a powerful Prosperity Stuffing:

- Loaf of bread
- I cup butter
- I medium onion, chopped
- 3 thinly sliced sticks of celery
- I½ teaspoons dried thyme
- I teaspoon ground sage
- I teaspoon rosemary
- Salt & pepper
- 2 cups of bone, chicken, or vegetable broth (if stuffing a chicken or turkey, then leave this out)

I. Let a loaf of bread of your choice air-dry overnight, then cut into I-inch pieces.
2. In a large saucepan, melt butter over medium heat.
3. Add onion & celery. Cook until onion is soft & translucent.
4. Mix in thyme, sage, rosemary, salt & pepper.
5. Add cubed bread & broth. Mix evenly.
6. Bake in a greased casserole dish at 350 F for 35-45 minutes.

The Taurus Ist quarter moon also supercharges all sorts of relationship spellwork as well, so be sure to share your meal with loved ones!

Magick for the Taurus Waxing Gibbous Moon

The waxing gibbous moon in Taurus can occur from November to May. At this time the sun can be in either Taurus, Gemini, Cancer, Leo, Virgo, Libra, Scorpio, or Sagittarius.

The waxing gibbous moon is the last stage before the full moon, and when we must trust that the intentions we set will come to fruition.

We can take the last steps we need to reach our goals & manifest our intentions. Any newly cast spells cast should require little turnaround time, as the constructive energies are reaching their peak.

Consider how they can help you with any intentions you set during the last new moon; Taurus's steadfastness can help keep us on track.

Be sure to wrap up spells that have been simmering over the course of the waxing phases before the full moon.

The waxing gibbous is a good time to recharge, and Taurus

loves luxury & low-effort magick. Don't be afraid to indulge your senses. Take a restorative soak in hot water steeped with rosemary, sage & thyme.

These all double as money-drawing herbs, and it is a good time to cast a quick prosperity spell. Fertile Taurus helps us to create abundance, especially during the waxing moon.

The Taurean moon is also a good time to cast any non-manipulative bonding magic, such as spells pertaining to trust, loyalty, friendship, bonding, or harmony in already established relationships.

This is also a great sign for pampering yourself and there's nothing better to celebrate earthy Taurus with than an indulgent — and beneficial — clay face mask.

Here's how to make it:

- 2 teaspoons of French green clay, bentonite clay, or Australian black clay
- I teaspoon almond or argon oil
- I teaspoon honey
- 2 drops each of rosemary, lavender & rose essential oils

Thoroughly, mix all ingredients together and apply to clean, dry skin. Allow mask to dry for I0-I5 minutes before gently removing with warm water. Pat dry with a soft towel.

Magick for the Taurus Full Moon

The full moon in Taurus occurs when the sun is under Scorpio — around the end of October & the beginning of November. As the Scorpio season spans from October to November, this means the Taurus full moon only occurs during one of these two months. If it is October the moon is the Hunter's Moon, but in November it would be the Beaver Moon.

In the Northern Hemisphere, it is autumn & the season of Samhain. If you enjoy using seasonal ingredients in your spellwork, look no further than one of fall's most recognizable symbols — the pumpkin. The seeds are excellent for jar or sachet spells, especially for fertility, beauty, growth, abundance, or protection spells.

Both seeds and whole pumpkins are good to have nearby when divining as they can provide more insight & clarity to your visions. For lunar spells, white pumpkins vibe the best.

Remember though that in the Southern Hemisphere, it is springtime & the season of Beltane. This means fresh flowers like daisies, roses & vervain are in season. They can be made into flower crowns to bestow clarity to visions, or the essential oils of these flowers can be used to anoint candles for divination work, which vibes with the full moon's energies — especially considering the sun's placement in Scorpio right now.

Heightened intuition comes naturally at the full moon, and we can use the moon's energy to amplify this further by drawing down the moon in a ritual. Usually done on a full moon, this ritual calls on the moon to fill us with her light & grant us clarity. It is traditionally done outside in the moonlight by chanting with raised arms.

The earth caught between the sun & the moon gives us the most powerful, all-purpose lunar energy in the moon's cycle, and the moon's energy is particularly potent under Taurus. Spells begun in Taurus can be next to impossible to stop & have lasting results.

Cast an easy earth spell under the full moon's light by drawing a sigil in the dirt outside your home for protection or to invite in prosperity.

Basil, mint, oregano, sage & thyme are all money-drawing herbs that are potent during a Taurus moon; their energies sync well together. Bundle them up & burn them to release their energies or use them in a sachet spell.

Or use those money-drawing herbs in the kitchen. Taurus loves indulging in physical luxuries, so delicious food is the perfect way to celebrate this full moon. Use your moon water to brew up tea or coffee. Or try using sigils in your kitchen magick; etch them into pie crust, draw them in your latte foam, or when you drizzle oil into a pan.

This full moon is also a wonderful time to celebrate & bless

long-term relationships. Cast spells for trust, loyalty,
friendship & bonding.

For bonding, bringing people together, and good eats, try
some basil pesto kitchen magick; it's just so good at bonding
people. And a good meal is an excellent way to bring people
together. It's hard to argue with someone when your mouth is
full of something yummy.

Here's a Basil Pesto Spell to bring out the best tempers at
your next gathering:

I. Toast a half cup of pine nuts in the oven at 350 F for
   about I0 minutes; flip halfway through. They will be
   lightly brown.
2. Then take the pine nuts, four cups of basil leaves, I/3
   cup of olive oil, and 2 cloves of garlic and process in a
   blender or food processor.
3. Add salt, pepper, and Parmesan cheese to taste. Can be
   stored in the freezer.

Magick for the Taurus Waning Gibbous Moon

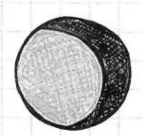

The Taurus waning gibbous moon occurs from May to November, meaning it can fall when the sun is in either Taurus, Gemini, Cancer, Leo, Virgo, Libra, Scorpio, or Sagittarius. Spells can be tailored to match the energies of both these signs.

With the moon in Taurus, spells pertaining to trust, loyalty, bonding & harmony in relationships are strong. The sun residing in either Taurus, Cancer & Libra can help amplify this, and the waning phases are the best for magick that repels, banishes & destroys things. Neutralize bad energy between people; try smoke cleansing with some basil, catnip, or lavender to do so.

Both the Taurus moon and the waning moon also aid in magick to dispel writer's block and bring creative inspiration, especially with the sun in Gemini or Leo. But if the sun is in an earth sign, like Taurus & Virgo, that links us to the material world, try destroying obstacles to prosperity & abundance instead.

Spell jars and sachets are easy ways to combine ingredients

to manifest your intentions, and there are numerous items that can be added to a jar or sachet for banishing, including black salt or crystals, like obsidian and black tourmaline;

Rue, rosemary & bay leaves are excellent herbal choices for this spellwork. Or you can use a cotton ball doused with a few drops of these herbs' essential oils instead. Crossroads dirt can also be added to open up roadblocks, or a key — after being cleansed — to symbolize doors opening.

To make a spell jar or sachet: first, choose your container and cleanse it. Saltwater or incense smoke are great ways to do this. Then set your intentions, you can speak them out loud, write them on a slip of paper to add to your container, or simply visualize them. After that, one by one add your ingredients, infusing them with your purpose as you do so. Seal & store on your altar until those intentions manifest.

The moon's energy is particularly strong during the Taurus moon, and spells begun in Taurus have long-lasting results. Spells cast under earth signs tend to be imbued with the element's endurance.

However, for the few days after the full moon, energies can feel sapped & slow as the moon recedes, and Taurus is very understanding of the need for rest after the full moon.

Magick for the Taurus Last Quarter Moon

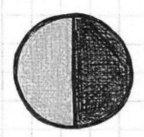

The Taurus last quarter moon can occur from May to November, which means the sun can reside in Taurus, Gemini, Cancer, Leo, Virgo, Libra, Scorpio, or Sagittarius.

The waning moon occurs from the moment the moon begins to fade from the full phase until it disappears once more; the last quarter moon is the halfway point between them & the energies are excellent for pushing away what we do not want.

Taurus & Virgo's energies help us to destroy any obstacles on your path to success. Harness the protective & money-drawing aspects of basil & sage. Bundle up the herbs & burn. Black thread is the best for banishing.

Another easy way to use earthen energies to banish something that has been bothering you: choose a crystal that brings balance & aids in letting go. Morganite, smokey quartz, or hematite are all excellent choices.

Then go to a quiet place and whisper your troubles to it — be specific. After you're finished, take the stone far from home

& bury it. Let the earth negate the bad energy you loaded into the stone.

If you can't find a good crystal to use, simply write your troubles down and bury them instead!

During the Taurus waning moon, neutralize bad energy from bad people in your life. Crystals like rose quartz & amethyst promote friendship & compassion — try setting up a crystal grid. Or dispel writer's block & bring creative inspiration by meditating in the moon's waning light.

The last quarter moon is an excellent time for cleansing as well. Relaxing & reflecting in a hot shower or bath is very in sync with the energies of this moon. Let what no longer serves you be washed down the drain.

Rock salt lamps vibe with Taurus' earthy energies and have many cleansing & protective properties as well; set one by your computer if you spend a lot of time online, or let your phone bask in the light of the lamp to cleanse bad energy that the devices might be holding on to.

Remember that the moon's energy is particularly strong under Taurus; spells can have long-lasting results.

Grounding is also an excellent activity that is heightened when the celestial bodies move through an earth sign like Taurus. Reconnect to the earth, by walking barefoot through the dirt and allowing your energies to flow into the ground.

Magick for the Taurus Waning Crescent Moon

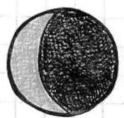

The waning crescent moon in Taurus occurs from May to November, meaning it can happen when the sun is in either Taurus, Gemini, Cancer, Leo, Virgo, Libra, Scorpio, or Sagittarius.

The waning crescent is a powerful time for casting bigger banishing spells & casting out anything you no longer want in your life. This close to the dark moon is when these energies are at their strongest. Release anything and everything that isn't serving you.

The waning Taurus moon is good for any banishing spells pertaining to relationships of all kinds. Use a cord-cutting ritual for a very permanent way to rid yourself of someone toxic. Or put Taurus' earthen energies to work by burying a poppet of whomever you need out of your life.

The smell of oregano helps you forget past lovers. So, do yourself a favor & order a pizza! Sprinkle the dried herb, which is also a delicious seasoning, over your slice & banish all memories of that person for good!

Money spells also are extra potent under fertile Taurus. This sign helps us to create abundance. Focus the waning moon's energy towards banishing financial woes.

In general, the moon's energy is rather powerful under Taurus. Spells begun in Taurus have long-lasting results & can be difficult to contain once set in motion. The sign's earth energy likes permanence, so be sure this works well with what you cast!

Another easy way to work with Taurus' earthy energies is with a lump of clay. Clay was one of humanity's first tools for sculpting the world around us, and it is still an excellent tool for any witch to use to manifest their desires.

Keeping in line with the waning moon's energy, mold your clay into something that symbolizes what you want to banish — sculpt a figure or etch a name into the clay. Imbue it with your intent & let it charge in the moonlight. Then, take your creation outdoors and stomp on it! Utterly destroy it!

♊ Gemini Magick

RULING PLANET: ☿
Mercury

SPELLS FOR:
communication
dreaming & divination
healing
travel
creativity
education

TAROT:
the Lovers
queen of cups
knight of swords
8,9,10 of swords

AIR MAGICK: △
Under an air sign, like Gemini, the moon amps up magick involving feathers, knots, or your voice.

Air's elemental direction is east.

The element of air is associated with wands or ceremonial blades.

CRYSTALS:
citrine, fluorite, malachite, peridot, clear quartz, agate, emerald & aquamarine

HERBS:
mint, burdock, dill, yarrow, tansy, heather, catnip, vervain, lavender, valerian, sage, skullcap & marjoram

Magick for the Gemini New Moon

The new moon in Gemini occurs with the sun also in Gemini — around the end of May & the beginning of June.

Be warned, Gemini's energies are quite scattered & spells are not always successful under this airy sign — not a terrible thing though, as it is best to refrain from major spellwork when the moon is truly dark. It is a better time to prepare for the upcoming lunar cycle.

Practice some spellwork to aid in introspection & reflection, including self-growth, recharging, or renewal. Embrace the laziness of the Gemini moon — do what you can and don't force your rituals.

Remember to take time during the new moon to set intentions for the upcoming lunar cycle. Dream big! Make a list of what you need to do to set your dreams in motion. Tarot or oracle cards can be used as guidance.

The new moon is the best time for new beginnings and new

ideas & education flourish under scholarly Gemini. Use the energy to study, research, or learn something new.

Gemini is extremely intellectual & curious beyond belief. Channel these energies with stones like agate & moonstone.

Agate enhances mental function & concentration, while moonstone provides inspiration and is a great crystal for new beginnings. Keep them nearby while you study or take notes!

Mercury, Gemini's ruling planet, also rules speech & the written word, making this a fantastic time for writing incantations or spells for future workings. It also means that speaking intentions aloud is quite powerful with both the sun & moon in Gemini.

Connect with the written word & journal or use it in your spellwork. The color ink you choose can help manifest a particular intention. Black ink is great for banishing or protection, while green is great for growth or wealth.

Use the moon as inspiration & the energy of Mercury to spend a late night writing or creating art. Not artistic? Try a pre-made kit from a craft store!

Air magick is potent right now, making spellwork with string a great idea! The premise of knot magick is simple: to bind your intention to the thread. Use rope, thread, yarn, wire, ribbon, or even hair & focus your energy into the cord.

Knot magic can easily be cut, burned, or untied to release the energies back into the universe. Undo the knot and undo the spell.

The element of air is also associated with wands. Weather

permitting, it is a lovely time to collect wood for a wand. Traditionally, only fallen wood should be used, and it is common to ask permission or leave an offering to the tree when gathering branches for ritual use.

Divination, dreaming, and prophecy also come naturally under Gemini. Harness this sign's dreamy energy by tucking herbs in a sachet under your pillow to inspire magickal dreams. Vervain and lavender vibe very well with Gemini, but mugwort & chamomile are also great choices.

It is a great time to read tarot or oracle cards. Relax & listen to the world whisper to you. Signs and revelations come in many forms; crows on the corner or street signs.

Answers can be found in many ways including tea leaves, working with pendulums, candles, dreamwork, scrying, casting runes, and more.

Cleanse & charge a book — a dictionary works very well — to use as a divination tool; perfect for a Gemini moon considering the sign's love of words. Ask your question & with your eyes closed flip open your book and point on the page. Examine the words, as they should hold your answer. If the message doesn't seem clear, reword your question — try being more specific — and ask again!

Gemini encourages us to seek out answers, so do it!

Magick for the Gemini Waxing Crescent Moon

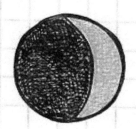

The waxing crescent moon in Gemini occurs from December to June, meaning the sun will be under Sagittarius, Capricorn, Aquarius, Pisces, Aries, Taurus, Gemini, or Cancer. Spells can use the energies of both celestial bodies, or just the moon, but the waxing moon is ideal for constructive magick.

However, spells are not always successful under Gemini as it is a fickle sign, and when the sun is in Gemini or Aquarius, the double hit of air energy doubles the fickleness that this element brings.

On the other hand, when the sun is in an earth sign, such as Taurus or Capricorn, spellwork is more grounded & longer-lasting, though slower in its results. If the sun is in an earth sign, try using the entire waxing cycle for a larger working to use those grounded energies.

This is the perfect time to start research or take a new class — sate Gemini's curiosity & drive for knowledge. Rosemary is known to stimulate memory, using a sprig as a bookmark can help you retain information while studying!

Yellow candles with scents like sage, jasmine, or tangerine give a powerful boost to confidence, creativity & optimism — perfect for Gemini's vibes. Not at home? Wear yellow jewelry,makeup, or clothing while out in public, and perfumes or essential oils with the same scents.

Gemini also throws out serious creative vibes. Take time to work on your creative pursuits. Staying busy also helps to dispel Gemini's nervous energy!

The waxing Gemini moon is also a great moon for drawing in good luck and works well with Gemini's vibes. Light a candle for luck and make some mint tea; the herb grants luck. Stir your drink clockwise to summon! Or if you're over 2I, brew & sip mint juleps by muddling mint leaves into whiskey and sprinkling in a little bit of sugar.

Inspire magickal dreams by burning mugwort & sage — or hanging the herbs in bundles near your bed if you can burn herbs where you live or are sensitive to smoke. Divination, dreaming & prophecy come naturally during the Gemini moon.

Put Gemini's elemental energy to use by cleansing with song or sound. And don't forget that speaking your intentions aloud is incredibly powerful!

Incantations can be self-written, or you can borrow from books, poems, psalms, song lyrics — or even a meme. Any words will work as long as they resonate with you & your intent.

Magick for the Gemini
First Quarter Moon

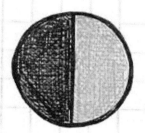

The first quarter moon in Gemini occurs from December to June. This means that the sun will reside under Sagittarius, Capricorn, Aquarius, Pisces, Aries, Taurus, Gemini, or Cancer, and the energies of those signs should be considered in spellwork as well.

For example, spells for communication flourish with Gemini, Aquarius, or Sagittarius empowering the sun & moon. In general, the waxing moon is excellent for spells that pull our desires towards us. These energies are at their peak during the quarter moon and it is a good time to take action towards manifesting any intentions you set at the new moon.

However, Gemini's vibes can be fickle & chaotic. Try using burdock to help combat that. Add the burrs to spell jars or burn with other incense to help your spells 'stick'.

The waxing Gemini moon is great for drawing in good luck. Anoint & burn a green candle with mint oil. Or bathe in mint & marjoram; their energies sync well with the Gemini moon.

Changeable & intangible, the element of air has moods & can embody many things. Think of how dreamy steamy showers are versus the cleansing strength of the wind at the beach. The wind can bring different properties to spellwork based on its direction, temperature, or even humidity.

And as air is a quick-moving element, harness it when you need instant energy in your spellwork.

Divination & dreaming come naturally during the Gemini moon. Cancer, Pisces, or Aquarius are also great signs for the sun to be in for this work! Harness the dreamy energy of Gemini by tucking mugwort, lavender, catnip, or chamomile into a sachet, and then placing it under your pillow to inspire magickal dreams. Selenite, moonstones & amethysts are great crystals to add to a dream sachet too!

The Gemini moon is a good time to study or learn something new. In fact, any spells for education, writing, travel, language, or ideas vibe well under this intellectual sign.

To help open your path to travel, take a white feather to a tall point on a breezy day and set it adrift on the winds.

Healing & medicinal work is also good in Gemini.

Magick for the Gemini Waxing Gibbous Moon

The waxing gibbous moon in Gemini occurs from December to June. This means that the sun will reside under either Sagittarius, Capricorn, Aquarius, Pisces, Aries, Taurus, Gemini, or Cancer. Spells can be tailored to match the energies of both signs.

Intellectual Gemini empowers spells for creativity, writing & ideas. The sun can be in one of several signs that vibe well with this energy too, including Sagittarius, Taurus, Aquarius, Pisces & Gemini!

The waxing gibbous moon, in particular, helps us to stop feeling burnt out & to recharge. So, harness the waxing moon's energies & get inspired creatively. Build a sanctuary to get the ideas flowing. Ring yourself in crystals & candles. Set the mood for creating.

Never underestimate the power of the senses either. Rosemary & spearmint are known for their uplifting scents and ability to clear the mind. Though essential oils should not be used

directly on skin, they can be diluted with a carrier oil to
safely do so! However, there is always an allergy risk when
working with new oils, so treat them with caution!

Here is a simple aromatherapy recipe for mental clarity:

- I tablespoon dried rosemary, crushed
- 5 drops lemon essential oil
- 5 drops of spearmint essential oil
- I cup carrier oil, such as olive or grapeseed oil

A dab of this mixture on either temple can help stimulate
creative juices, and it can be sealed & stored for later use.

Divination, dreaming & prophecy also sync naturally with the
Gemini moon. Harness this dreamy energy with herbs like
mugwort, vervain, lavender, catnip, or chamomile. Burn them
or use them in a bath.

The waxing Gemini moon also is a great moon for drawing in
good luck, learning something new, and healing work.

The time of day should also be considered when casting.
Healing & divination both vibe with Gemini's energy, but
sunrise & early morning empower healing, while divination is
best done at night.

Just remember that spells are not always successful under a
Gemini moon, as the energies of this sign can be restless!
However, keeping busy can keep those energies at bay.

Magick for the Gemini Full Moon

The full moon in Gemini occurs with the sun in Sagittarius. The Sagittarius season spans from November to December, which means the Gemini full moon only occurs during one of these two months. If it is November then the moon is the Beaver Moon, but in Decemberber it is considered the Cold Moon.

The energies of both Gemini & Sagittarius make this a fantastic time for spells for communication & creativity.

Use the full moon to bless your book of shadows, journals, or writing tools. Or connect with the written word by making homemade ink. Ink can be made from a number of things, but brown ink can easily be made from a common household item — tea! Here's how:

- 4-5 bags of black tea
- I teaspoon vinegar
- I teaspoon gum arabic
- 2 drops thyme essential oil
- I/2 cup boiling water

I. Pour water over the tea & allow it to steep for about I5 to 20 minutes.
2. Add the gum arabic & stir. It is important to note that the water should be hot when it is added & the tea mixture may need to be reheated to do so properly. Keep stirring until the mixture reaches a nice even color.
3. Add the vinegar to set the color & strain.
4. Add a few drops of thyme essential oil before bottling, as it will naturally inhibit mold from growing.

Use this magickal ink to write in your book of shadows or for any spellwork that requires writing as well.

This is also a great time to cleanse bad vibes from your phone, computer, or other communication devices. Valerian & clove make a great combo for jar & sachet spells to provide protection from gossip & other malicious energy. Or set black tourmaline on your phone at night to soak up negative vibes.

Divination, dreaming & prophecy all come naturally at the full moon, and both Sagittarius & Gemini are in sync with these energies as well. Emotions, intuition & creativity are heightened at this time.

Angelite & celestite are perfect crystals for air signs. Oozing divination & healing energies, they are powerful in dreamwork. Add them to sachets or dreamcatchers for this inquisitive moon — just so as long as you're willing to go down the rabbit hole!

Use this dreamy energy to charge tarot cards, runes, or other divination tools. It's also a great time for readings. Relax and listen to the world whisper to you. Mugwort & mint tea will send you into another world. Inhale the vapors deeply & sip. You only need a little!

Use caution, as mugwort is a powerful plant, and only ingest in small doses. Would-be moms & those with allergies should avoid it completely!

Healing work is also good in Gemini. Use the moon's power to make homemade herbal medicines like elderberry syrup or thyme-infused honey.

Gemini's energies are very scattered. Spells cast during a Gemini moon are not always successful because of this fickle nature. Dispel Gemini's restless energy by staying busy. Gemini hates being bored.

Magick for the Gemini Waning Gibbous Moon

The waning gibbous moon in Gemini occurs from June to December. This means the sun will be in either Gemini, Cancer, Leo, Virgo, Libra, Scorpio, Sagittarius, or Capricorn at this time.

This phase is best for magick that repels, banishes & destroys, pushing away what we do not want. However, for the few days after the full moon, energies can feel sapped & slow as the moon recedes, making it a good time for introspection.

This is a great time for journaling, as Gemini loves the written word. Any spells for education, writing, travel, language, or ideas flourish under this sign. Virgo & Sagittarius are great signs for the sun to be in to further amp up this energy.

The energies of Mercury can be used as a guide for writing & other creative endeavors, which can also be incorporated into spells. Write down obstacles you face on a bay leaf & burn them with nettles & sage.

Did you know that you can cleanse your tools & trinkets with nothing but your own voice? Breath & the spoken word are exceptionally powerful under Gemini, and the waning moon is a great time for cleansing.

Write a short poem or chant to recite over your tools — or look one up! The power is no less. Then use your breath to blow away any energy clinging to the item. Remember: it is the will that makes the witch, not the wand. You are the most powerful tool you will ever need!

Spells cast during a Gemini moon are not always successful, as the sign is quite chaotic. Prioritize what needs to be done as thoughtlessness & unfocused energy can cause spells to fail.

Yet, you can use this sign's love for the written word to your advantage, as journaling, and especially mood tracking, can focus your energy & help you flow with Gemini's chaos.

Blue is the color of trust and communication; choose to write in blue to remove barriers & blocks in communication, as well as prevent misunderstandings.

Banishing bad luck, poor health, or self-doubt all vibe well with the energy of the waning Gemini moon too.

Magick for the Gemini Last Quarter Moon

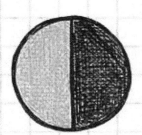

The last quarter moon in Gemini occurs from June to December, so the sun will reside either Gemini, Cancer, Leo, Virgo, Libra, Scorpio, Sagittarius, or Capricorn at this time. And the energies of both celestial bodies can be harnessed into spellwork!

Spells cast during a Gemini moon are not always successful. However, the waning phases have the best energy for spellwork that banishes or destroys. Just be ready to combat the restless energies that come with working under this sign.

And Gemini is totally a sign of curiosity, chaos & communication. But a bit of simple magick can block drama & bad energy: slip a scrap of paper with a sigil into the back of your phone case.

Divination works well with this moon too, but in the waning phases, look to the past for answers rather than divine the future. It is a good time for pendulum work, tarot readings, or rune readings.

You can you the waning moon's energy & Mercury's influence over communitcation to stop gossips by writing the person's name or the rumor itself on a fresh valerian or mullein leaf, both of which are vague tongue-shaped. Then, roll up your metaphorical 'tongue' into a tight tube shape, and secure it with metal pins to bind the tongue of the gossiping offender.

Or use Gemini's energy to banish illness & injuries! Healing & medicinal work is good in Gemini, adding an extra oomph to herbal salves, tinctures & syrups. Here's a simple recipe for a healing spell that stores well; candied ginger to banish motion sickness, morning sickness & other bellyaches:

- 5 cups of water
- I pound fresh ginger, sliced and peeled
- I pound raw cane sugar

I. Combine water and ginger in a saucepan and cook over medium heat until ginger is tender; about half an hour. Remember to stir counterclockwise to banish!
2. Strain mixture. Save ¼ cup of liquid.
3. Return ginger and water to a saucepan and add sugar.
4. Bring to a boil, stirring frequently.
5. Reduce heat & cook until sugar crystallizes.
6. Separate pieces and transfer to a drying rack. Store in an airtight container for up to 2 weeks. Freeze up to 6 months.

Magick for the Gemini Waning Crescent Moon

The waning crescent moon in Gemini can occur multiple times from June to December. This means the sun will reside either in Gemini, Cancer, Leo, Virgo, Libra, Scorpio, Sagittarius, or Capricorn Use the energies of both the sun & the moon in your spellwork.

For example, Virgo & Gemini amp up healing work. Harness the waning moon's energy to banish illness by making homemade healing salves, tinctures, or a medicinal herbal tea!

Leo, Libra, Gemini & Sagittarius all work well in banishing blocks in your creative energy. Lemongrass can be burned for this purpose. Use the moon as inspiration & the energy of Mercury as a guide for writing & creative endeavors.

Keep in mind that the waning crescent phase is a powerful time for casting banishing spells, releasing emotions, rituals for cleansing, or spells seeking to destroy. This close to the dark moon is when these destructive energies are at their strongest.

As the waning crescent is an excellent time for cleansings & the wind can be employed to cleanse ritual objects, especially sea breezes. Under Gemini, air magick is quite powerful. Knot magick, wands, fans, feathers, or your breath can also be utilized.

The crescent moon's destructive energies can be put to use by taking a pair of scissors to thread. Use the thread to tie two things together symbolically; photos, locks of hair, or paper with your purpose more fully written out. Then, use the scissors to permanently sever that connection.

Writing with a feather quill is also a great way to tap into Gemini's intellectual & elemental energies. Feathers can also be used to flesh out a protective circle before casting, and white feathers in particular represent air signs.

Try to speak your spells aloud to tap into that elemental power — it's incredibly powerful! Or find a breathing app to help with meditation before a ritual!

Your breath can also be used to blow out your candles, rather than snuffing then, in order to let the element of air reign.

♋ Cancer Magick

RULING PLANET:
The Moon

SPELLS FOR:
protection
motherhood & fertility
divination & dreaming
emotional healing
cleansing

WATER MAGICK: ▽

Under a water sign, like Cancer, the moon amps up magick involving water; especially any natural water like the ocean or rain.

Water's elemental direction is west.

The element of water is also associated with cauldrons or chalices.

TAROT:
the Chariot
king of wands
queen of cups
2,3,4 of cups

HERBS:
dandelion, sage, jasmine, chickweed, clove, hyssop, chamomile, anise, lemon balm & rosemary

CRYSTALS:
moonstone, opal, calcite, selenite, chalcedony, pearl & turquoise

Magick for the Cancer New Moon

The new moon in Cancer occurs with the sun also in Cancer, around the end of June & the beginning of July, meaning it is just about Midsummer — at least in the Northern Hemisphere.

Spend the long summer days wildcrafting & harvesting herbs for your spellwork — it is a fantastic time for it.

Remember in the Southern Hemisphere is it the opposite time of year, making it close to Midwinter & Yule. In folklore, both oak & holly are associated with both Yule & Midsummer, and both are great to include in your altar decor & spellwork for the season.

Consider the possibilities of harnessing the summer sun's energy at the height of its power by charging water in the sunlight; particularly during Midsummer's Day at sunrise or noon. Moon water made during the winter solstice, the longest night of the year, is also equally powerful.

Both sun & moon blessed water have a variety of uses.

Adding food coloring to your moon water will help coordinate it to your intent. There are also a variety of edible glitters & iridescent powders that can be used as well — you know, for the aesthetic!

With both the sun & the moon in Cancer, this is an optimal time to cleanse & remove negative energies from the home. Washing your floors & thresholds with mint essential oils diluted in vinegar can chase out bad vibes, while smoke cleansing with herbs for bonding like catnip, lavender, or basil brings harmony into your home.

Or just clean up in general; nothing eases tensions around the house more easily than cleaning up a bit.

Add a bit of salt & rosemary essential oils to the detergent when washing your clothes for protection; create spiritual armor. Cancer is great for both spells involving water & domestic magick.

For one reason or another though, Cancer's energies are also usually emotionally charged. Self-pity & moon swings can cause spellwork to falter under a Cancer moon.

But it also makes this a great sign for healing, especially emotional trauma. Use meditation & simple spellwork, like bath rituals & smoke cleansing, to balance out the emotional volatility of the moon in Cancer. It can cause quite the fluctuation of feelings.

Since Cancer heightens intuition, it causes more sensitivity to the unknown, as well as emotions. In fact, divination comes naturally during the Cancer new moon — a perfect time for reading runes or tarot cards!

Cancer is also the most fruitful sign of the zodiac and a

good sign for green witchery, so be sure to work some plants
or herbs into your spellwork. Dig in the garden or go on a
wildcrafting walk.

Lemons vibe with Cancer's energy; their happy energy can
balance out the emotional volatility that Cancer brings. Use
fresh lemons for a drink that refreshes & uplifts the spirit:

I. Make a simple syrup. With IO cups of water and I cup of
   sugar, bring water to a boil in a saucepan & stir in sugar
   clockwise until it dissolves.
2. Let the mixture cool to room temperature, then chill.
3. While you wait, squeeze 2 cups of fresh lemon juice. You
   will need a couple dozen lemons. Strain out seeds & pulp.
4. When cold, add lemon juice to the water/sugar. Add ¼
   teaspoon of salt & stir!

Magick for the Cancer Waxing Crescent Moon

The waxing crescent moon in Cancer can occur from January to July. This means the sun will be in either Capricorn, Aquarius, Pisces, Aries, Taurus, Gemini, Cancer, or Leo.

Spellwork can focus on the energies of the moon, or work with the energies of the sun as well. Even seasonal energies can be considered; the waxing Cancer moon phases can occur multiple times from winter to summer, and those energies vary quite a bit throughout the year! Consider the possibilities of using snow & ice to tap into Cancer's elemental!

In general, Cancer's energy is highly charged emotionally, but it is a great sign for spellwork involving healing, especially emotional trauma. Start some serious healing work over the course of the waxing moon; eat better, journal, or start therapy. Do what you need to.

Cancer's dreamy energies can be used to foster restful sleep with the help of herbs or essential oils. Chamomile promotes sleep & eases anxieties, while rose softens grief, and

vetiver grounds the mind & dispels sensitivities. They can
easily be put to work in a scented pillow spray to promote
positive dreams & ease emotional tensions:

- 2 oz witch hazel
- I0 drops chamomile essential oil
- 5 drops vetiver essential oil
- 5 drops rose essential oil

I. Combine all ingredients in a small spray bottle & spritz
   onto your pillow, blankets, or pajamas before bed! Shake
   well before each use.

Engage in some self-care & harness the potent power of water
during a Cancer moon; try bathing in sage & thyme. Both are
herbs that promote emotional healing from past traumas.

Remove negative energies n & bring harmony into the home by
smoke cleansing with lavender & sage! If you can't have
smoke where you live or if you are sensitive to it, try using
essential oils & moon water in a diffuser!

To harness the Cancer moon's protective qualities, cast a
circle around your home. Wreaths of mugwort, posies, and
chamomile are also strong protection, and dried fennel can be
hung by doors & windows to ward away negative energy &
intentions.

A string of dried berries on a red thread can also be worn or
carried for protection. Rowan vibes well with Cancer. Keep
the charm on you for the entire course of the waxing phase to
continually draw in protective energy!

Magick for the Cancer First Quarter Moon

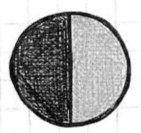

The first quarter moon in Cancer occurs from January to July, meaning that the sun will fall under Capricorn, Aquarius, Pisces, Aries, Taurus, Gemini, Cancer, or Leo. The energies of both the sun & moon can be put to work magickally.

For example, the energies of both Aries & Cancer work well with protection spells and protection spells for the home or children are especially potent under Cancer. If you're casting a protection spell for kiddos, be sure to include chamomile or elderberry! These plants are extra protective of little ones!

Aloe is a plant with energy that vibes well with Cancer's and dried aloe leaves can be burned as incense to invoke protection & wisdom. A dried aloe leaf can also be used as a talisman against misfortune & accidents; put them in spell jars or sachets.

Cancer is a great sign for healing, especially any emotional traumas, and Pisces & Gemini also amp up those powerful healing energies.

The energies of Cancer are often emotionally charged, and we can be left feeling lonely. Inspire compassion & connection with crystals like rose quartz or lapis lazuli; they can be easily carried in your pocket to do so.

Or foster good vibes at home and smoke cleanse with herbs that foster bonding. Basil, catnip & lavender all help us feel good and connected, while both sage and thyme help us to move on from past trauma.

Don't hesitate to call up your coven or surround yourself with the familiar. Be kind to yourself.

Dreaming & divination are also within the domain of the Cancer moon. Use any combo of lavender, chamomile, catnip, or mugwort to aid in calling down these energies. Try using them in a bath or as a tea as Cancer amps up water's energy.

Candle magick can still be potent under a water sign; the melting waxing represents water. To boost candle magick more, use floating candles in a dish of moon water.

Magick for the Cancer Waxing Gibbous Moon

The waxing gibbous moon in Cancer can occur from January to July. This means the sun will be in either Capricorn, Aquarius, Pisces, Aries, Taurus, Gemini, Cancer, or Leo at this time.

During the gibbous phase, there is little time to harness that energy before the full moon. Wrap up spells that have been simmering over the course of the waxing phases. Any newly cast spells should require little turnaround time, as the constructive energies are reaching their peak.

Use the Cancer moon to recharge your energy with a bath of lemon balm & rosemary. Water spells are supercharged under this sign and both lemon balm & Cancer are ruled by the moon.

Don't have a tub? Brew your lemon balm up into tea with honey & relax in the moonlight. The moon's element is water after all! Put it to work!

Emotions can be volatile with the moon in Cancer. The element of water aids us in expressing emotion & drawing out our feelings, but sometimes it can be too much! Moodiness can get in the way of not just your spellwork, but your life as well.

Respect Cancer's watery element & work through mood swings with a simple grounding spell; drop a stone into a body of water — a river, the ocean, your bathtub, a bucket, whatever feels right. Meditate with the stone beforehand, and when emotions hit hard later think about the gentle lap of water against the stone dispersing them.

This is also a great time to cast protection spells, especially for the home or children. Grow or cast with herbs like sage, mugwort & rosemary that can channel protective vibes. Chamomile & elderberry, in particular, work well for protection spells for kids.

Eggshells are also a great addition to protection spells; mix crushed eggshells with salt to use in protection circles.

Other spells that flourish under Cancer include: divination, dreaming, motherhood, fertility, and those for personal or emotional growth.

Magick for the Cancer Full Moon

The full moon in Cancer occurs with the sun in Capricorn, at the end of December or the beginning of January; right around the time of the solstice.

The Capricorn season spans from December to January. This means the Cancer full moon only occurs during one of these two months. If it is December, the moon is considered the Cold Moon, but in January it is the Wolf Moon.

Nurturing Cancer makes this is the perfect moon for blessings & protection spells for children & the home. Blessings can be performed anytime, but dawn is quite powerful for this work.

Ward your doors with bundles of herbs or an herbal wash; Cancer vibes well with rosemary, chamomile, or sage. Chamomile & elderberry, in particular, are known to watch over children. Just remember when handling any new plant that there is always an allergy risk!

Aloe vera gel can be used to anoint your brow or your tools before a lunar ritual to imbue them with that energy.

Magickally, chickweed is also an especially good herb for lunar rituals that also vibes well with Cancer. Add the dried herb to salt & sprinkle when casting a protection circle. Or dry & hang around your home in bunches for protection.

Divination also comes naturally at the full moon. Emotions & intuition are heightened, as we are tapped into the most powerful lunar energy in the moon's cycle. And Cancer heightens them to the extreme, causing sensitivity to the unknown as well.

Use meditation & simple spellwork, like bath rituals & smoke cleansing, to balance out the emotional volatility of the moon in Cancer. Put the sign's watery energy to use; find a natural body of water to dip your toes in while you meditate in the moonlight.

Moon water is an essential component of many spells & can be easily made. Simply put water in a clean glass container & seal. Visualize & state your intended purpose — this can be as simple as 'imbue this water with lunar energy' or something more specific. Then, leave it to charge for a few hours in the moonlight.

Moon water is used for a number of magickal purposes — add it to your essential oil diffuser or bathwater. Use it to make tea, coffee, or even ice. Extinguish your ritual fires with it. Or even cleanse your ritual tools with it. Herbs & water-safe crystals can also be added during the charging portion. And rain, sea, or river water can also be used to make moon water that will NOT be ingested!

The shore is also an immensely powerful place to perform rituals if you can find a secluded beach. The sand is perfect for a simple banishing spell; drawing sigils, names, or other symbols for the waves to wipe away. The full moon's energies can be used for constructive or destructive magicks & the tides can be employed for both.

Constructive spells are best done when the tide is moving towards us, from low to high. Conversely, destructive spells are best done when the ocean moves away from us, going from high tide to low.

For one reason or another, Cancer's energies are quite emotionally charged, which can cause quite the fluctuation of feelings. Self-pity & mood swings can cause spellwork to falter under a Cancer moon, so try to keep a level head!

Despite the emotional rollercoaster, the Cancer moon can send you on, it is a great sign for healing emotional trauma & bringing harmony into the home, making it an optimal time to remove negative energies in the home and calm drama between family members.

Burning herbs for bonding, like basil & lavender, is an easy way to achieve this. The oils of these herbs can also be put in a diffuser instead!

To celebrate the full moon & combat loneliness infuse fresh fruits & veggies, which have a magick of their own, into cold drinking water. Cucumbers, strawberries, oranges, or limes all taste delicious! Herbs can be added too; rosemary & lemon is a powerfully uplifting combination. Or, if you're of legal drinking age, infuse champagne to make sangria to lift the spirits — perfect to share with friends & family.

Magick for the Cancer Waning Gibbous Moon

The waning gibbous moon in Cancer can occur from July to January, meaning that the sun will reside in either Cancer, Leo, Virgo, Libra, Scorpio, Sagittarius, Capricorn, or Aquarius at this time.

The waning moon's energy is best put to use in spells that banish, repel & push away what we do not want. However, for the few days after the full moon, energies can feel sapped & slow as the moon recedes, making it a good time for introspection.

Still, this moon is a good time to cleanse your home & ritual tools, especially with the sun in Virgo or Cancer, but nothing major. Try washing your clothes with a bit of salt & rosemary essential oils for protection; create spiritual armor. Cancer is great for both spells involving water & domestic magick.

Cleanse the energy in your home. Cast out old beef & resentments. Absorb bad energy with a circle of sage and salt, or burn a bundle of herbs for bonding.

It is a good time to clean out your fridge & pantry too. Expired foods hold stale, negative energy, and sometimes those energies can permeate the whole kitchen! Just think about the smell of rotting produce — yuck!

After a fresh cleaning, put a mix of baking soda, dried rosemary, and a few drops of essential oils — cinnamon, clove, or lemon are all cleansing — in your fridge in an open container to absorb bad smells & energies. Leave in your fridge for up to 3 months before replacing.

Cancer can have us craving the feelings family brings — including our surrogate families! Call up your tribe & cook up a good meal. Kitchen magick vibes well with Cancer; a sign that's all about hearth & home.

Dreaming and divination also come naturally during a Cancer moon, but during the waning phases look inward & into the past for answers rather than the future.

Magick for the Cancer Last Quarter Moon

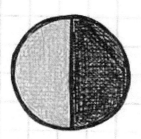

The last quarter moon in Cancer occurs from July to January. This means that the sun resides in either Cancer, Leo, Virgo, Libra, Scorpio, Sagittarius, Capricorn, or Aquarius. Your spellwork can be tailored to the energies of both signs.

For example, Scorpio, Sagittarius & Aquarius all lend their energies to divination & prophetic dreams. And Libra helps Cancer balance emotional energy & create domestic harmony, while Cancer & Virgo have cleansing energies.

The Cancer waning moon's energy creates an optimal time to cleanse & remove negative energies from the home. Wash floors & thresholds with a mint & vinegar rinse to chase out bad vibes. Or banish turmoil in the home by spending some time smoke cleansing.

Use meditation & simple spellwork, like bath rituals & smoke cleansing, to balance out the fluctuation of emotions that Cancer brings. Vetiver, associated with the element of earth, is an especially grounding aroma and can help balance intense emotions & calm oversensitivity. Diffuse it through your home if Cancer has you feeling overwhelmed.

Or channel Cancer's domestic vibes & practice some kitchen magick. Try making some herbal butter with sage or rosemary. These protective herbs vibe very well with this zodiac sign. Garlic bread is also easily imbued with garlic's protective properties — and it can be shared!

Sigils are also easily incorporated into your kitchen magick; etch them into pie crust or draw them in your latte foam.

Keep in mind that the waning phases are most conducive to magick that repels, banishes, or destroys. Spells involving water are potent under Cancer. Have a friend, relative, or coworker that is giving you a hard time?

Get them to chill out by writing their name on a scrap of paper and submerging it in a small cup of water. Then, put it in the freeze to metaphorically freeze the person's actions against you. Just remember to use a paper or plastic cup, as glass can shatter when the water expands!

Magick for the Cancer Waning Crescent Moon

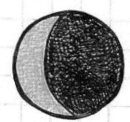

The waning crescent moon in Cancer can occur from July to January. Therefore, the sun can reside in either Cancer, Leo, Virgo, Libra, Scorpio, Sagittarius, Capricorn, or Aquarius.

The energies of both those signs can be channeled into spellwork as well; Sagittarius has great energies for truth spells and Libra loves revenge. Or you can choose to focus on the moon's energies.

The waning crescent phase is a powerful time for casting bigger banishing spells. It can occur in Cancer multiple times in a single year, oftentimes falling in the height of hurricane season. The strong storms that occur this time of year can be used for strong banishing magick, using the elements of water & air to do so. Let the storm carry away a symbol of what you want to release. Take care not to venture outside in any bad weather as it can be extremely dangerous. It is much better to set up your spells before the start of the storm.

So under the Cancer moon, banish past traumas & other blocks to your emotional healing, as it is the best sign for healing emotional traumas & bringing harmony into the home. Neutralize bad energy from bad people and get rid of anything that makes your safe space uncomfy!

Use Cancer's elemental energies; a glass or bowl of moon water can be left by the door of your home or room to trap negative energies from coming home with you. Touch your fingertips to it before entering and leave your worries at the threshold. Be sure to change the water frequently, so stagnant energies & bacteria don't build up!

Cancer's energies also aid in spells for protection & seawater has powerful protective & healing properties. Drip some around your doorways & windows to block negativity. Seashells are also excellent for use in protection spellwork & vibe with Cancer's watery element.

The waning moon's energies are also great for cleansing rituals; take an herbal soak with salt & purify yourself & your energy. Or bathe in herbs for harmony — chamomile & lavender are a great combo — and banish bad emotions down the tub's drain. Let the water carry it away. Mood swings can cause spellwork to falter under a Cancer moon. Don't let your emotions get the best of you!

Leo Magick

RULING PLANET:
The Sun

SPELLS FOR:
self-confidence
sex & love
leadership
creativity
strength
courage

HERBS:
cinnamon,
poppy, vervain,
sunflower,
St. John's wort,
lemon balm,
rosemary,
chamomile
saffron
& rue

TAROT:
Strength
king of wands
knight of pentacles
5, 6, 7 of wands

FIRE MAGICK: △

When the moon resides under a fire sign, like Leo, magick involving fire, incense & candles can be very powerful.

Fire's elemental direction is south.

The element of fire is also associated with wands or ceremonial blades.

CRYSTALS:
amber, topaz, ruby,
tiger's eye,
calcite,
diamond
& citrine

Magick for the Leo New Moon

The new moon in Leo occurs with the sun in Leo as well, between the end of July & the beginning of August. In the Northern Hemisphere, this is just after the height of summer and about the season for Lughnasadh.

Corn is symbolic of this season & is used for both decor & offerings during this time. Many people have a tradition of making dolls from cornhusks during the harvests, which are used as charms to bring prosperity & well-being to the home.

On the other side of the world, it is the opposite time of year and around the season of Imbolc. Cornhusk dollies are also traditional for this festival too, although you can use corn or cornhusks in spells for abundance, prosperity & luck any time of year!

The double Leo energy wants our heart in our work. Leo wants us to reconnect with our passions — what makes us burn — and to share them with the world. Set aside time for creative ventures or pursuing your passions, and remember that when the moon is truly dark in the sky, it is a better time for introspection & reflection rather than casting anything huge.

Yet, the Leo moon makes it an excellent time for casting spells pertaining to whatever you are passionate about — and, yes, that includes love spells! Write the name of your desired on a slip of paper & fold it around a rose quartz crystal — for unconditional love. Burn a pink or red candle anointed with crushed thyme & rose petals over the bundle. Let the wax seal the paper around the stone to seal in the energies while the moon waxes.

Just remember strong love & binding spells can be harmful & manipulative! A self-love or self-confidence spell puts out better energy, but in the end, it's up to you to decide how to put your magick to work! Instead, try brewing up a lemony tea with lemon balm to encourage self-love & happiness; this herb vibe with Leo's sunny energy! Stir clockwise to summon confidence & charisma for yourself.

A delicious lemony dressing to inspire happiness & good vibes can be made using ginger, lemon slices & lemon balm. To make, fill a sealable jar 3/4th full with dry plant material and cover with apple cider vinegar. Store in a cool, dry place & shake lightly daily. After 4 weeks, strain out the plant matter. Store in a cool, dry place and use as you would any vinegarette.

As Leo is ruled by the sun — the only sign ruled by the sun — it is a great time to use ingredients that resonate with the sun, like lemons and other citrus. You can also charge water or salt in the afternoon light to create solar salt, which can be used in magick for positivity, creativity & more. This new moon is the perfect time to make it, as the moon is resting, and the summer sun has only just begun its wane.

Fire signs grant creative energy too; put together a sachet or jar spell to channel that creative force! Lemongrass, rose petals, lavender, clove, citrine & tiger's eye are all excellent additions.

Glitter can be used to color-coordinated your intent too, yellow or blue work well for creative spells, and glitter vibes well with Leo's penchant for drama as well. You can also add cold charcoal or ashes to symbolize the element of fire in your jars & sachets — and not cause a fire hazard!

Of course, lighting candles when casting is an easy way to harness the double Leo energy of this new moon; fire magick is extra potent right now. Or host a bonfire for your coven! Leo is a super social sign after all.

Don't forget to trim your candle wicks as well. It's important for air quality and they can be used in other spellwork to represent fire.

Magick for the Leo Waxing Crescent Moon

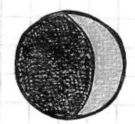

The waxing crescent moon in Leo occurs from February to August. This means the sun can fall under Aquarius, Pisces, Aries, Taurus, Gemini, Cancer, Leo, or Virgo. You can use the energies of both celestial bodies in your spellwork.

Spells for magick that pull our desires towards us are potent under the waxing moon. Leo & Aries make a great combo to summon charisma & courage, while spells for sex, love & passion pair better with the sun in Taurus or Leo.

You can use the course of the waxing moon to cast a major binding spell. Try braiding, knotting, or weaving your intentions into black thread. Be careful though, binding spells are strong magic. These spells can be harmful & manipulative; use caution when casting.

A safer bet is a self-love spell, which is also great to cast during the waxing moon, or a less direct love spell. Try keeping a crystal or two, like garnet or rose quartz, in your pocket to attract love rather than bind a specific person to you. Vervain, thyme, or rose essential oils are great perfumes to inspire affection. Just be sure to use them with a carrier oil before any skin contact!

The Leo waxing moon is also a good time to summon your creative energies; Gemini, Virgo, Taurus & Pisces are all great signs for the sun to be in for creative work. Leo wants us to reconnect with our passions and what makes us burn.

Set aside time for creative hobbies; draw, dance, make music. Do what makes your heart happy! Burn yellow or orange candles to bring creative energies into your space while you work.

If possible, it is always better to let your candles & ritual fires burn to completion rather than putting them out — not always doable though.

So with both the sun & the moon under a fire sign, try to snuff out your candles and fires if you safely can rather than blowing them out. Blowing out candles is an act of empowering the element of air, and should be saved for when the celestial bodies are in one of the air signs.

Remember though, the energy of fire signs like Leo is best put to use in spellwork that requires rapid results, but not long-lived ones.

Magick for the Leo First Quarter Moon

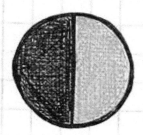

The first quarter moon in Leo can occur from February to August, meaning the sun will be in either Aquarius, Pisces, Aries, Taurus, Gemini, Cancer, Leo, or Virgo. Channel the energy of both the sun & the moon into your spellwork — or don't! And focus on the moon instead!

The energies of both the first quarter phase & the moon in Leo are fantastic for spellwork to strengthen relationships of all sorts, particularly animal magick. So pamper your pets & familiars. Give your kitties some catnip to thank them for their friendship, or howl at the moon with your hound!

Leo is a very social sign, in many senses. Rituals to gain influence with people, increase social status, or imbue charisma are all in sync with Leo's energy.

Feeling up to making some new friends? Let Leo guide the way with some candle magick. Burn a rainbow of candles — a pack of birthday candles is perfect — around a piece of rose quartz to welcome friendship into your life. This is especially potent when the sun is in either Aquarius, Gemini, or Leo.

And, of course, spells for love, passion, sex & binding spells do vibe with Leo's energies, as it is a sign that is all about power & pleasure.

Summon up seductive energy by stuffing a jar or sachet with herbs like basil, lavender, cinnamon, or rose petals and a token of your would-be love — a picture, a few drops of their perfume, or their name written in red ink — to keep under your pillow or in your purse. Crystals like carnelians & garnets are also great additions.

The Leo moon is a good time for spellwork to enhance your creative passions as well. Moon water made under the waxing moon imbues it with creative & inspirational energies — perfect for this sign.

But be aware that enthusiasm & overconfidence can cause spellwork to falter while the moon is in Leo. Stay patient & humble; no one is perfect and this includes you. Take the extra time to burn a black candle before any major spellwork to clear any negativity & protect your intent.

Magick for the Leo Waxing Gibbous Moon

The waxing gibbous moon in Leo occurs from February to August. This means the sun will be under Aquarius, Pisces, Aries, Taurus, Gemini, Cancer, Leo, or Virgo. And the energies of those signs can also be considered in spellwork.

For example, passionate Leo grants us creative energy & Gemini, Virgo, Taurus or Pisces can all lend their energies towards spellwork that bestows creativity. Set aside time for creative hobbies & what makes you happy.

This is a good moon phase to rest & recharge; Leo loves luxury & the self. Taurus vibes with this as well, so if the sun happens to be in Taurus then all the better! Journal, meditate, or take time for yourself however you see fit!

Fight self-esteem issues & self-doubt. Bathe with herbs that boost your confidence and that vibe with Leo's sunny state of mind. Try sunflower, chamomile, or calendula. Ring the tub as you soak with as many candles as you can & harness Leo's elemental energy.

Clusters of aragonite around the tub can help attract
feelings of self-worth & self-confidence. Just be careful
with this crystal around water, as is not safe to get it wet.
This is true for most crystals that end in "-ite", but others
as well. Always double-check which crystals can be submerged
before casting with water.

Another option is a glowing honey mask glamour spell to
bestow confidence, charisma & courage:

- I tablespoon raw honey
- I tablespoon oat flour
- I/2 teaspoon rosewater, witch hazel, or moon water
- I-2 drops each of calendula & patchouli essential oils
- Pinch of dried calendula

Mix all ingredients thoroughly & apply to face for I0-I5
minutes. Rinse & pat dry.

Remember though, that same confidence that Leo grants, can be
your spellwork's undoing!

Leo also enhances love spells, which are also great to cast
during a waxing moon. Just be sure to avoid manipulative
magic, as it can come back to bite you!

For example, you can use a tarot or oracle card to represent
a specific person or relationship, which can be manipulative,
versus using it to represent the type of person you wish to
attract.

Magick for the Leo Full Moon

The full moon in Leo occurs with the sun in Aquarius. The Aquarius season spans from January to February, which means the Leo full moon only occurs during one of these two months. If it is January, then the moon is considered the Wolf Moon, but if it is February it is called the Snow Moon.

Aquarius shows us our place in the world, a cog in the mechanisms of society, while Leo reminds us how essential every cog really is.

Reconnect with your passions and what makes you burn. More importantly, share it with the world. Both Leo & Aquarius help us do this. Celebrate yourself, cultivate your talents, and shine!

The full moon gives us the most powerful lunar energy in the moon's cycle. Use the sun & moon's combination of celestial energy to call down the sun, and supercharge a self-confidence spell using chamomile, calendula & sunflowers in a bath — all herbs that vibe with Leo.

A splash of moon water can aid in charging your bath, and floating candles in the water is an aesthetically pleasing way to incorporate the element of fire into the ritual.

Just watch out, as the enthusiasm & overconfidence Leo brings can be the downfall of your spellwork.

The moon in Leo can also cause us to dramatize our lives & seek attention, which is not always a bad thing. A bonfire ritual or other social gathering vibes well with Leo and can help release that energy.

Try tossing herbs for prophecy into the flames, like yarrow, mugwort, thyme, or bay leaf, and gazing into the flames. Divination comes naturally at the full moon, and emotions & intuition are heightened too.

An excellent sign for love or sex spells, Leo & pleasure go hand in hand. Touch is a strong element to include in any love spell, and a massage bar makes a wonderful love spell to use later with your partner:

- I tablespoon beeswax
- 2 tablespoons olive oil
- I tablespoon shea butter
- I0 drops rose essential oil
- 5 drops lavender essential oil
- I tablespoon dried rose petals
- I tablespoon coffee beans or adzuki beans

1. Melt shea butter, olive oil, essential oils, and beeswax in a double boiler on low heat, and mix well.
2. Add beans & dried herbs to the bottom of your mold
3. Pour heated mixture into the mold, and transfer into the refrigerator to harden.

You can test the consistency easily by hardening a sample in the fridge for a few minutes and rubbing it between your fingers until you are satisfied. Add beeswax to stiffen and oil to soften to find the right consistency.

To use, melt the bar slightly between your palms before gliding it over your skin, or your partner's.

Lore claims that gifting your lover a medallion or necklace of moonstone on the full moon will grant you a passionate relationship. You can even plan on charging it in the full moon's light to imbue it with Leo's passionate energy.

Masturbation, orgasm & sex magick can also be employed to help summon a lover, although this can lead to a relationship that does not progress beyond anything sexual. Whether or not you want that is up to you!

Magick for the Leo Waning Gibbous Moon

The waning gibbous moon in Leo occurs from August to February, which means that the sun can reside under Leo, Virgo, Libra, Scorpio, Sagittarius, Capricorn, Aquarius, or Pisces.

Consider how you can incorporate the energies of both celestial bodies & their signs into your work, and that the waning phases are best for magick that pushes away what we do not want. Pisces or Sagittarius can help Leo banish blocks in creativity, while Scorpio & Libra vibe well with Leo's penchant for passion, sex & love.

Banish blocks in motivation, creativity, self-confidence, or your love life by first burning a black candle — for banishing — on your altar followed by another candle of a corresponding color to your intentions. Yellow or orange can be used for creativity or confidence, while pink or red can be used for love or passion.

Alternatively, charge up a spell by lighting a black candle each day of the waning phase to burn away & banish what's getting in the way of your success, particularly in sports, performances & creative ventures. Under Leo, candle magick & spells involving fire are very potent.

Sage, bay, rosemary & rue are all excellent herbs to use for banishing spells. Eggshells also have powerful banishing & protective properties. Save & wash your eggshells to grind up for later spellwork.

However, for the few days after the full moon, energies can feel sapped as the moon recedes, making it a good time to relax before any larger workings. A bath ritual can help us recharge during this phase, and you can imbue your bath with the energy of the sun, which rules Leo. Add water or salt charged in the sunlight to do so.

Chamomile, basil, lemon balm & rosemary all vibe with Leo's sunny energy. If you don't have a tub, hang your herbs on the showerhead to activate their energies with steam. Just remember to remove them before they get moldy!

Magick for the Leo Last Quarter Moon

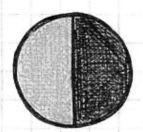

The last quarter moon in Leo occurs from August to February, meaning that the sun can reside under Leo, Virgo, Libra, Scorpio, Sagittarius, Capricorn, Aquarius, or Pisces at this time. You can use the energies of both these signs to fuel your spellwork or work with the moon alone.

Seasonal energies & spell ingredients can also be considered; the waning Leo moon phases can happen several times from early fall into winter, and those energies can vary quite a bit throughout the year!

The waning moon's energies are very strong during the last quarter moon, and they are best used for magick that banishes & destroys. Harness that energy to be rid of obstacles in romantic pursuits.

Leo is an excellent sign for any love or sex spells — this is especially so with the sun in Leo, Libra, or Scorpio. Pink & red candles are great choices for these types of spells, but the shapes of the candles can be chosen for what they

represent as well — especially if you make them yourself!
Heart or roses are perfect for love spells!

Tea brewed with thyme can bestow passion and grant the
courage to overcome obstacles to love, while burning
lemongrass & bay can destroy those obstacles. And of course,
Leo, as a fire sign, amps up magick involving candles or
other flames, so using fire in your banishing spells is a
wonderful idea!

Leo is also the best sign for fighting self-esteem issues &
banishing self-doubt. The waning Leo moon can be used to
banish laziness, fear, and dependency.

Burn an offering of homemade incense to cleanse your own
negativity. Using a mortar & pestle, grind down dried
patchouli & cedar for confidence & personal strength. Then,
burn over a charcoal disk in a fire-safe dish.

Keep a couple of stones in your pocket to surround you with
their energy — sunstones grant luck, independence &
fearlessness, while tiger's eye keeps us confident.

Just remember that with the moon in Leo, too much confidence
& an inflated ego can easily make your spellwork falter.

Magick for the Leo Waning Crescent Moon

The waning crescent moon in Leo occurs from August to February. This means that the sun can reside under Leo, Virgo, Libra, Scorpio, Sagittarius, Capricorn, Aquarius, or Pisces. Spells can be tailored to match the energies of both these signs.

The waning crescent is a powerful time for casting bigger banishing spells & casting out anything you no longer want in your life, as well as releasing energies that aren't serving you. Under Leo, release arrogance & pride as they can block your spellwork's success.

Self-confidence spells are very powerful under the Leo moon & the waning moon aids in ridding ourselves of the obstacles to confidence. Place crystals like pink tourmaline by your mirror to promote self-love & acceptance, or amazonite to refresh your spirit. Rose quartz can even help heal your broken relationship with yourself!

Lemon balm, chamomile, and mint are great for mending the spirit and instilling self-confidence. Sit, soak, and then let all the bad juju get washed down the drain. And if the sun happens to be in Pisces, well, it vibes especially well with bath magick!

The element of fire is quite potent under fiery Leo; super-charge your bath ritual with as many candles as you can find. Think of how lovely the tub will look by candlelight — just use caution!

Put Leo's dramatic flair to use with a rather showy banishing spell; in a relatively open space, take a ⅓ cup of vodka or other strong spirit & pour it into a cast-iron cauldron. Swish gently counterclockwise. Then, step back and, with caution, toss in a lit match.

The alcohol should ignite immediately & with fervor, so use extreme caution & have a method to put out the flame nearby. That flame can then be used to burn paper or bay leaves with your intents written on them. The waning Leo moon is excellent for banishing creative blocks, fear, dependency & more.

Passionate Leo is also an excellent sign for love or sex spells. As the moon is waning, it is also a great time to end relationships. Break things off with someone for good with a banishing or cord-cutting spell. Or use the waning moon's energy to break barriers between lovers.

♍ Virgo Magick

RULING PLANET:
Mercury

SPELLS FOR:
communication
material gain
career success
cleansing
healing
writing

EARTH MAGICK:
Under an earth sign, like Virgo, the moon will enhance magick involving crystals, stones, salt, dirt, or roots.

Earth's elemental direction is north.

The element of earth is also associated with pentacles & besoms.

TAROT:
the Hermit
queen of swords
knight of pentacles
8,9,10 of pentacles

HERBS:
mint, chamomile, fennel, thyme, lavender, skullcap, heather, savory, aster, marjoram & valerian

CRYSTALS:
jasper, turquoise, peridot, amethyst, fluorite, jade, tourmaline & agate

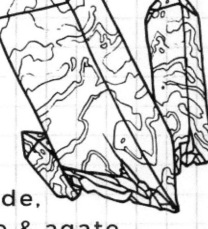

Magick for the Virgo New Moon

The new moon in Virgo occurs with the sun also in Virgo, around the end of August & the beginning of September.

This double dose of Virgo energy is great for planning & preparing spells that require great detail, though when the moon is truly dark in the sky, it is best to refrain from major spellwork. It is a much better time to prepare for the upcoming lunar cycle, but Virgo's energy can be harnessed into any task that needs considerable focus.

However overthinking, meticulousness & self-criticism can stand in the way of spells cast under Virgo. Cut yourself a little slack & be kind when mistakes happen. Virgo has us seeking perfection & sometimes the cost is more than we bargained for.

Virgo also fills us with an intense need to cleanse & the new moon is associated with cleansing & new beginnings, making this the perfect time to brew an anointing oil for future spells & rituals. A dab of oil can cleanse a candle, blade, or other ritual tools of negative energy or — if made using skin-safe oils — dotted on the third eye for mental clarity. Here's how to make a New Moon Anointing Oil:

In a small jar, combine the following ingredients & charge under the new moon.

- 3oz jojoba, olive, or other carrier oil
- I moonstone small enough to fit in the bottle
- I/2 teaspoon crushed rosemary
- I/2 teaspoon black or sea salt
- 9 drops of lavender essential oil
- 9 drops of sage essential oil

This is also a good sign for self-care. Take advantage of the Virgo moon's vibes by relaxing in a bath of lavender & chamomile. Add the herbs directly into hot water or use essential oils instead. Purifying salts are a great way to use the earthen element in your bath ritual — or even salt scrubs!

Salt scrubs are easy to make too. Simply combine I0-I5 drops of your preferred essential oils — lavender, mint, or chamomile all vibe well with Virgo — with I/4 cup skin-safe carrier oil like coconut, jojoba, or olive oil, and a cup of sea salt. Mix before each use, as the salt & oil can separate.

Put the element of earth to work further & ring your tub with crystals while you soak. Just take care that you don't put your crystals in danger — not all of them are water safe!

Earth magick is potent right now; crystals can cleanse a space's energy or add peaceful vibes to your bath ritual. Jasper in particular vibes well with Virgo & grants a sense of tranquility while absorbing bad energy.

Or try setting up a crystal grid to manifest your intentions. Clear quartz matches just about any intention and is known to help amplify your energy, making it an ideal tool to use.

Grounded Virgo is great for spells that exist in the material world. Earth signs imbue practicality. It is a good time for spells to improve success in your career or to attract funds.

Bury a dollar bill in the pot of a mint plant to encourage your funds to grow. Getting your hands dirty is a great way to tap into Virgo's earthy energies.

Never grown herbs before? The new moon is a perfect time to try something new!

Earthen energy is best put to use for spells that simmers over a long period. It grants your magick endurance & steadiness.

Magick for the Virgo Waxing Crescent Moon

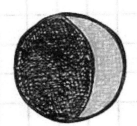

The waxing crescent moon in Virgo can occur multiple times from March to September. The means the sun is in either Pisces, Aries, Taurus, Gemini, Cancer, Leo, Virgo, or Libra during this time. The energies of both celestial bodies, as well as seasonal energies, can be considered when casting.

Virgo basks in the tedious. The waxing crescent Virgo moon is a good time to begin complex magic that needs to simmer over the course of the moon's cycle. Cast any spells that require great detail & ample time; Virgo is a great sign to start anything complicated.

It is the perfect time to sit down and start working on a skill or begin a class that might help you achieve success at work or in your future career. Harness Virgo's energy into a task that needs focus.

Virgo also fills us with a need to clean & cleanse; the home, ourselves, our ritual tools & our spirits. Use mint & mugwort tea to cleanse sacred spaces & objects. Take a rag & dust with the brew, or flick it lightly over your altar.

Cleansing your candles, especially store-bought, is never a bad idea either. Anoint them with oil or use herbs like sage & mugwort to smoke cleanse.

Earth signs link us to the material world & the waxing phases are perfect for constructive magick of all sorts; spells for magick that pulls our desires towards us. The energies of both Virgo & Taurus are in sync with money-drawing spells.

Keep jade in your pocket to attract wealth. Or add the stone to a sachet with thyme, marjoram & mint; all-powerful money-drawing herbs that work well under Virgo. Tie it off with a green or gold string!

Or infuse a meal with love, luck, and abundance by roasting a bulb of fennel under a Virgo moon; fennel & Virgo vibe well together. All you need is the bulb, olive oil, and balsamic vinegar. Here's how:

I. Slice the bulb into quarters.
2. Drizzle with olive oil and balsamic vinegar.
3. Roast at 400 F for 40 minutes. The edges will be nicely caramelized when they are finished.

Magick for the Virgo First Quarter Moon

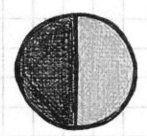

The first quarter moon in Virgo occurs from March to September, which means the sun will reside in either Pisces, Aries, Taurus, Gemini, Cancer, Leo, Virgo, or Libra. The energies of both those signs can be channeled into spellwork.

If the moon & sun are both in earth signs, use crystals to cast a protective spell around your home. Simply bury a protective gem, like black tourmaline, at each of the four corners of your home!

Taurus & Pisces vibe well with spells for cleansing, as well as material gain, while Libra & Gemini can aid Virgo in spells for communication.

Virgo & Gemini together are a particularly great combo for spellwork involving writing. When you journal, write down your plans, or add a written intention to a spell consider the color of the ink you are writing with & how it vibes with those intentions.

Green, gold, or even brown ink are great for spellwork for

material gain or wealth, while orange is excellent when looking for career success.

The waxing moon is for constructive magick, such as attracting wealth & positivity. It is a good time to accomplish the tedious & work on projects, as Virgo keeps us to be reliable & mindful of routine. Organize. Plan for success.

This is the perfect sign for focusing on the practical details of life; try sticking to a new diet or exercise plan. Draw a rune on your wrist or hand to remind yourself to focus when working on a big project.

Any & all complex magick thrives under Virgo; work on spells that require great detail. Just be aware that overthinking & self-criticism can stand in the way of spell cast under Virgo.

Virgo is also a good sign for grounding rituals & cleansings. In fact, Virgo fills us with a deep need to cleanse. Take advantage of the Virgo moon's vibes by relaxing in a bath of herbs that can help ground & rebalance. Sage, rosemary & nettles help to center & ground. Add herbs directly into hot water or use essential oils — and don't forget to add salt to your tub!

Magick for the Virgo Waxing Gibbous Moon

The waxing gibbous moon in Virgo occurs from March to September, meaning that the sun resides in either Pisces, Aries, Taurus, Gemini, Cancer, Leo, Virgo, or Libra at this time. Tailor your spellwork to fit the energies of both celestial bodies — or don't and simply focus on the moon!

The waxing gibbous moon is the last stage before the full moon & when we must trust that the intentions we set will come to fruition. It is time to take the last steps we need to reach our goals & manifest our intentions.

During the gibbous phase, any newly cast spells cast should require little turnaround time, as the constructive energies of the waxing phases are reaching their peak. There is little time to harness that energy before the full moon.

This is also when you should wrap up any spells started at the beginning of the waxing cycle. Virgo is great for spells that require great detail, so ending a long spell under a Virgo moon is a great idea!

Cut everyone, including yourself, a little slack. Be kind when mistakes happen. Virgo has us seeking perfection, sometimes at the cost of those around us. Diffuse oils or burn a scented candle — lavender & vetiver are both calming & grounding — to help release that perfectionism.

The waxing gibbous does give us the energy to refocus, something Virgo is good at. After Virgo's relentless push to get things done, brew a cup of mint tea to recharge, relax & be rid of stress.

This is the perfect sign for focusing on the practical details of life. Grounded Virgo is great for spells that exist in the material world: cleansing & self-care. Take time to organize and clean your space.

Earth magick is also potent right now. Carve a charm from a piece of sturdy root or paint a stone with a sigil. Clay is also an excellent medium for making amulets, runes & other magickal tools.

Crystal grids are a great way to channel those elemental energies & manifest as well. The multiple stones can really amplify your intentions. However, if you don't have the time or energy to set an entire grid up, just carry a crystal in your pocket instead!

Magick for the Virgo Full Moon

The full moon in Virgo occurs with the sun in Pisces. As the Pisces season spans from February to March, this means the Virgo full moon only occurs during one of these two months. If it is February the moon is known as the Snow Moon, but in March it is considered the Crow Moon.

The full moon occurs when the earth is caught between the sun & the moon. This gives us the most powerful lunar energy in the moon's cycle. Emotions, intuition & creativity are all naturally heightened during the full moon. And these powerful energies can be used in many ways, but both Pisces & Virgo fill us with a need to clean and cleanse — our home, our ritual tools, ourselves, and our spirits.

Purify yourself in a bath with sage, rosemary & lavender. Cleanse your phone; delete apps, old photos & texts. Wipe it down. Banish bad energy with a sage & rosemary smoke cleanse.

Our clothing can also become bogged down with bad energy. Wash clothes with aromatic essential oils & a pinch of salt to cleanse on a deeper level.

Ritual objects can be easily cleansed with earthy energy using baths of salt. Simply immerse the tool in a bowl filled with sea salt. Selenite bowls are excellent for this, as this crystal has immense purifying properties. Selenite crystals can also be placed on or around just about anything to absorb the object's bad energy.

A besom — a broom made up of a bundle of foliage around a central stick — is another symbol of earth, and they can be used in a myriad of ways, including cleansing & warding. Traditionally, besoms were made with an ash handle, birch bristles, and willow wood cording — all sacred trees — but there are many store-bought options available to the modern witch. They can also be easily made from found materials. Herbs like mugwort can be used as bristles.

Besom handles can be made using a good-sized stick. Your bristles can be easily wound around one end and secured tightly with a cord. The stray ends at the top of the bundle of bristles can be carefully folded over the cording, so they are facing downward & tied off once more. Plant stems can often be soaked overnight to make them more pliable to work with too! Once made, they can be blessed underneath the full moon — clothing optional!

It is also a wonderful time to journal, which can be quite emotionally cleansing & healing! Experiment with different colored inks to help set intentions & release emotions. Black ink is perfect for banishing, and red can summon romance. Try orange to draft a resume or blue to calm tensions with someone you are struggling with.

Try harnessing the healing energies of both Virgo & Pisces, as they are both excellent signs for healing work. Charge your healing crystals in the light of the full moon. Other divination tools benefit from charging in the moonlight as well! Don't forget about your tarot or oracle cards, candles, pendulums, runes, etc.

Remember when you are charging a crystal or other ritual tool you are imbuing it with energy for later use, versus cleansing a crystal or other object, which is the act of removing old, stagnant energy from that object. Both are important for spellwork, but shouldn't be confused!

Virgo is especially good for spells that require great detail; such as more complicated thread magic, cooking, or intricate sigils — Virgo favors work with sigils. Remember when casting that, the earthy energies of Virgo grant the endurance & stamina necessary for long-term success.

It is also the perfect sign for practicing discipline & focusing on the practical details of life. Try sticking to a new routine. Draw a sigil on your wrist or hand to remind yourself to focus.

Yet, overthinking & meticulousness can stand in the way of spells cast under Virgo, so don't drive yourself crazy seeking perfection or trying to get something just right!

Magick for the Virgo Waning Gibbous Moon

The waning gibbous moon in Virgo occurs from September to March. This means the sun can reside under either Virgo, Libra, Scorpio, Sagittarius, Capricorn, Aquarius, Pisces, or Aries at this time.

Seasonal energies & spell ingredients can also be considered when casting; the waning Virgo moon can occur multiple times from autumn into early spring, and those energies can vary quite a bit!

This phase is conducive to magick that repels, banishes & destroys things, pushing away what we do not want. You can use the entire waning cycle to work some big magick.

Forgo a single-day spell for one that takes more time & intricacies. Virgo's earthy energy is practical & patient, preferring the slow & steady wins the race method. It gives our spellwork the stamina to simmer over a long period. Think incremental growth!

Harness Virgo's energy into a task that needs considerable

focus or patience. Vanilla extract is a staple for any kitchen witch, and nothing beats homemade! It's also quite the lesson in patience, as it can take several months to complete — a perfect project for Virgo's vibes. Here's how to make it:

I. Cut 3-6 vanilla beans in half longways.
2. Fit the beans into an airtight glass jar & cover with 8oz of plain 80 proof vodka.
3. Seal & store in a cool, dry place. Shake weekly. It should be ready in as little as 8 weeks, but for a stronger flavor, it can be left to simmer up to I2 months.

Just remember that for a few days after the full moon, energies can feel sapped & slow as the moon recedes, making it a good time for rest introspection rather than any major casting. It is a good sign to do some journaling, learn something new, or start a routine!

Start a garden, even just a single potted plant, and get your hands dirty. Work with magickal & medicinal plants. Obtain some fresh herbs from the garden or the grocery store. It doesn't matter which! Spend some time drying or planting them while Virgo empowers the moon's energies.

As an earth sign, Virgo charges earth magick, and the routines of watering & weeding are very grounding.

Magick for the Virgo Last Quarter Moon

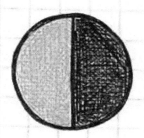

The last quarter moon in Virgo can occur from September to March. Therefore, the sun will reside in either Virgo, Libra, Scorpio, Sagittarius, Capricorn, Aquarius, Pisces, or Aries.

The waning phases are best for magick that repels, banishes, or destroys, making it a good time for dealing with temptations & banishing bad habits. Virgo's energy has us striving for perfection & helps us not to waver in our convictions. It's the perfect sign for practicing discipline.

The Virgo waning moon is an excellent time to shed chaotic vibes & organize. Channel Virgo's meticulous energy into a task that needs focus.

Mercury rules Virgo, as well as speech & the written word. Writing & saying incantations for spellwork works well with Virgo's energies. This is especially true if the sun happens to be in an air sign like Libra or Aquarius, which will further empower the energies of your voice.

Virgo & Mercury also amp up work with sigils and designing

your own can be quite easy! Write a simple intention on a piece of paper, then cross out any vowels or repeated letters. Break down the remaining letters into their fundamental lines.

Enjoy rearranging those lines into an abstract sigil that calls to you. There's no right or wrong way to do it! That sigil can then be drawn where it can be put to use. Draw them in your candles or on your wrist. Sigils can be placed under phone cases or at thresholds for a myriad of uses!

Virgo also fills us with a need to clean ourselves and our spirits. So, purify yourself with a bath with sage, rosemary & lavender. A bath can double as some self-care, which Virgo also loves. Salt is an easy way to incorporate the element of earth into your bath rituals.

As an earth sign, Virgo vibes with magick that harnesses that element. Crystals, dirt, or clay can all be considered for potential use in spellwork too!

Since Virgo thrives on the tedious, it is a great sign to set up a more complicated crystal grid as well. Use the waning moon's energy & crystals like smokey quartz or obsidian to banish & unblock. Flower petals, bones, runes & more can also be incorporated into the grid!

Magick for the Virgo Waning Crescent Moon

The waning crescent moon in Virgo occurs from September to March, meaning the sun can reside under either Virgo, Libra, Scorpio, Sagittarius, Capricorn, Aquarius, Pisces, or Aries. Use the energies of both celestial bodies in your casting, or choose to focus on the moon's!

In general, this is a good time for cleansing & banishing bad energy. Virgo loves to organize, clean & cleanse, so banish chaos & filth from your home.

Take the time to tidy up or purify yourself with a sage, rosemary & lavender bath. Smoke cleanse your phone, as well as delete old photos & texts. Ruled by Mercury, Virgo is a sign of communication, so using the waning moon's energies to cleanse your communication devices is a great idea. Placing them near selenite, salt, or even a rock salt lamp can use Virgo's earthy energies to help achieve this.

Any spells cast during the beginning of the waning phase should be wrapped up before the dark moon. The energies Virgo provides are excellent for ending a complicated spell, as the sign's earthy energies give our spellwork the patience & endurance to do so.

Use the moon's energy to add an extra oomph to herbal salves, tinctures & syrups. Virgo is great for banishing illness, and the waning phases are best for magick that repels, banishes & destroys. This close to the dark moon is when these energies are at their strongest.

Try making a health sachet or jar spell for yourself or a loved one. Use a lock of hair, a photo, or a tarot card to represent the person it is for, and add healing & protective herbs or crystals to give it power. Ginger, sage, rosemary, eggshells, agate & salt are all common ingredients. Give it as a gift or bury it under the light of the moon.

Just remember that overthinking can stand in the way of spells cast under Virgo. Aromatherapy can help release some of that perfectionism & stop overthinking. Lemon, ginger, or mint are all great choices!

Libra Magick

SPELLS FOR:
love & relationships
balance & cooperation
justice & revenge
self-confidence
beauty & the arts

RULING PLANET:
Venus

AIR MAGICK: △
When the moon is residing under an air sign, like Libra, magick involving feathers, knots, or your voice is very effective.

Air's elemental direction is east.

The element of air is also associated with wands or ceremonial blades.

TAROT:
Justice
king of cups
queen of swords
2,3,4 of swords

HERBS:
thyme,
burdock,
clover, raspberry,
apple blossom,
bergamot, thyme
nettles, yarrow,
elderberry & lavender

CRYSTALS:
morganite, rose quartz, diamond, opal, ametrine & lapis lazuli

Magick for the Libra New Moon

The new moon in Libra occurs with the sun also in Libra, around the end of September or the beginning of October.

This places the timing near the fall equinox in the Northern Hemisphere & the spring equinox in the Southern — either way it is a time of ultimate balance. Don't forget to take these seasonal energies into account when making offerings or choosing spell ingredients.

Use the double Libra energy to generate balance & as a chance to slow down. Try using celestite in your spellwork. It's a stone of balance that grants the mental clarity & harmony that Libra craves.

Remember when the moon is truly dark in the sky, it is often best to refrain from major spellwork. Although work involving introspection, recharging & reflection isn't a bad idea!

The new moon is also when you should set intentions for the upcoming lunar cycle. Visualize your goals and figure out what you need to manifest them. Make a list of what you need to do to set your dreams in motion. Tarot or oracle cards can be used as guidance. Refocus your path & ask hard questions. Under Libra, a sign of air & communication, ask your questions aloud if possible. Just be prepared for the answer!

Libra gives us an awareness of how other people see us. Imbalances can become obvious when we haven't taken the time to assess ourselves. The Libra moon is a good time for a look at our relationships & how we connect to each other.

Groupwork & partnerships also thrive under Libra. Cooperation & teamwork can lend power to spellwork.

Take time to meditate, reflect & use the power of your breath; air magick is potent right now. Try cleansing your space with sound — bells or even your voice work well — or craft a playlist for your new moon ritual.

It is also a good time for aromatherapy or smoke cleansing under an air sign like Libra. Open your windows and burn rosemary & yarrow for protection & purification, or meditate under the new moon with lavender & chamomile in your essential oil diffuser to aid in reflection & rebalancing.

Knot magic is wonderful for the beginner witch & it is associated with the element of air. The materials are easy to gather and the premise is simple: to bind your intention to the thread. A quick spell can be a simple knot, while knitting, crocheting, or weaving can be used for larger works.

And if something doesn't work out, in general, all you need to do is undo the knot to undo the spell.

Spells pertaining to the delivery of justice are best done in Libra, including revenge spells. But beware, Libra serves justice where it is merited. If you're at fault be prepared to come to terms with it.

Nails, pins, or a few drops of vinegar can be put in a jar with hair, a photo, or some representative of the person the spell is focused on. Add a written note for specifics & don't be afraid to speak it aloud first. And hell, I wouldn't be afraid to spit in it as well. Seal with black wax & bury.

But beware, vinegar & iron in a sealed jar are extremely dangerous! Together, the two create fumes that will eventually build up & explode, creating a literal bomb. Avoid this combo when choosing your ingredients.

Spanish moss is also a great ingredient in revenge & justice spellwork. It can be used to stuff pillows or poppets, and it's a neat alternate material to use in knot magick.

Just be careful as Spanish moss can harbor insects! If you are harvesting it yourself it is a good idea to sterilize it when bringing it indoors! Boiling is a common method, but it is also easy to dampen it & microwave in 30-second intervals.

Magick for the Libra Waxing Crescent Moon

The waxing crescent moon in Libra can occur from April to October. Therefore, the sun will be in either Aries, Taurus, Gemini, Cancer, Leo, Virgo, Libra, or Scorpio. Both the energies of the sun & moon can influence spellwork.

When the sun is in Libra or Gemini, the double hit of air energy makes it a good time for fast & more immediate spells, but also redoubles the fickleness that this element brings as well. Contrastingly, when the sun is in an earth sign, such as Taurus or Virgo, spellwork is more grounded & longer-lasting, though slower in its results.

If the sun is in an earth sign, try using the entire waxing cycle for a larger working to use those grounded energies. Light a stick of incense every night until the full moon & use Libra's energies to summon compromise & cooperation. Libra is happiest with everyone living in harmony.

The Libra moon can also be used to attract love & beauty. Try a bath ritual — Scorpio is a great sign for the sun to be in for this. Rose petals, lavender, thyme & catnip are all great for this type of spellwork, and vibe well with Libra's energy too. Don't forget salt & a splash of moon water!

You can also tie an article of your clothing to something of your partner's to create a bonding charm. Just make sure you pick something they won't miss! If the knot comes undone, so will the spell!

Place a crystal on top of your face cream or foundation to transfer its energy. Rose quartz attracts love, while tiger's eye grants courage. Or anoint your mirror with a confidence-boosting wash of cinnamon, orange & catnip essential oils diluted in moon water.

It's also a great time to try any spells involving legal matters, righting past wrongs, or anything that needs to be balanced a little better.

Use the waxing moon to summon success in a court case or bring about a positive outcome. Dress an orange candle in crushed bay leaves — both attract success & promote positive thinking — by rolling the candle first in olive oil & then the crushed leaves. Etching a rune or a short word like 'WIN' into the wax can help channel your intent further.

Light it and visualize your ideal outcome. If possible, let the candle burn completely out.

Magick for the Libra First Quarter Moon

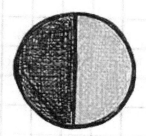

The first quarter moon in Libra occurs from April to October, meaning the sun can reside under Aries, Taurus, Gemini, Cancer, Leo, Virgo, Libra, or Scorpio at this time. Remember to take the energies of both signs into account as you work.

For example, the first quarter moon supercharges all sorts of relationship spells, and Libra, Leo & Scorpio also aid in spells involving love & couples.

The waxing Libra moon is also a good time to cast glamour spells, conjure beauty & summon self-confidence. Hang herbs for beauty like bergamot, chamomile, or lavender — which are all in tune with Libra's energies — on the showerhead to activate with the steam. Just remember to remove them before they get moldy!

For a quick beauty spell, splash your face with a balancing witch hazel toner to bestow confidence & generate balance:

- 2 oz witch hazel
- 2 oz rose water

- IO drops lavender essential oil
- IO drops chamomile essential oil

Combine all ingredients in a small spray bottle & shake well before each use. It can even be stored in the refrigerator for a cool morning spritz.

Or try a lavender & bergamot hair mask before a hot shower for shiny hair; both these herbs promote peace & relaxation. Mix 2 drops each of lavender essential oil & bergamot essential oil to 2 tablespoons of olive oil. Heat in the microwave until warm & massage into hair. Leave on for I5-20 minutes & shampoo out afterward.

Bergamot also aids in bringing clarity to visions, and alongside mugwort makes an excellent incense to burn when doing a tarot reading. As a sign all about balance, Libra wants us to put the active energy of the waxing quarter moon into harmonizing our lives with the grand design. It is a perfect time to ask big questions during your readings.

Any spells pertaining to legal matters, righting past wrongs, revenge, or the delivery of justice are also best done in Libra, but the scales serve justice where it is merited. If you're at fault, beware.

Magick for the Libra Waxing Gibbous Moon

The waxing gibbous moon in Libra can occur from April to October. This means, during this time, the sun will be in Aries, Taurus, Gemini, Cancer, Leo, Virgo, Libra, or Scorpio.

The energies of both those signs should be considered in spellwork, as well as seasonal energies. The waxing Libra moon can occur several times from spring into autumn, and those energies vary throughout the year!

Libra sends out some nurturing vibes for an air sign. Use them to rebalance, recharge & engage in some self-care. Meditate or try some yoga. Take a nap or have a good snack! Taurus & Cancer are both great signs for the sun to be in to add to that nurturing energy too!

On the other hand, Gemini, Leo, or Aries amp up the creative energies of Libra, and Libra loves beauty & creating beauty. Work on your creative pursuits or harness the waxing moon's energy to cast a glamour spell or summon beauty; bathe in lavender & honey.

You can also put your makeup to work magickly. Use concealer to metaphorically conceal self-doubt. Or color co-ordinate lipstick or eyeshadow to your goals; red for love, green or gold for wealth & money, or black to ward off bad energy.

Libra is also the ultimate sign for casting spells related to justice or revenge — consider the possibilities with both the sun & moon under the sign of the scales.

The Justice major arcana card can be used in spellwork for just that. A lodestone placed with the card on your altar helps to summon a just resolution to a quarrel.

Like any air sign, Libra rejoices in the written word & spoken. Repeating affirmations in the mirror is an especially potent way to tip the scales in your favor. Speaking your intentions aloud during a ritual is incredibly powerful — it's a simple way to harness Libra's elemental energies.

Remember though, that air is often chaotic & fickle and it can interfere with spellwork! Casting when the sun is in an earth sign like Taurus or Virgo can help add longevity to important spells.

Magick for the Libra Full Moon

The full moon in Libra occurs with the sun in Aries. This means the Libra full moon only occurs during March or April. If it is March, the moon is considered the Crow Moon, but in April it is the Pink Moon.

The season of the ram has us plowing forward at full speed. Use the Libra full moon to combat this and generate balance. It offers a chance to slow down for some self-care. Imbalances can become painfully obvious when we haven't taken the time to slow down and assess ourselves & our lives.

Libra also gives us an awareness of how other people see us. Allow the truth to change you. Try consulting with your tarot or oracle deck to further your insight, or confirm what you might already be aware of. If you're looking for a sign, that is already the sign you need!

This is a good time to confront changes in our relationships and how we connect to each other. Banish obstacles for healthy partnerships & relationships. Smoke cleanse bad vibes with lavender & sage. Inspire bonding with your partner with an herbal massage bar or even a good meal.

Any spells involving couples, righting past wrongs, or anything that needs to be balanced a little better work well at this time. On the flip side, Libra will also serve justice where it is merited. If you're at fault with something be prepared to come to terms with it.

Libra also loves beauty & harmony. It is THE sign of aesthetics, so try a beauty spell when the moon is in Libra. Grind down the petals of red roses with a mortar and pestle to make a natural blush-slash-beauty-spell.

Hang herbs for beauty like bergamot, elderflower, chamomile & lavender on the showerhead to activate their energies with steam. Just remember to remove them before they get moldy! Or infuse them in a bath or in a facial steam.

Divination comes naturally at the full moon. However, Aries' energies can be an impediment to it. Emotions & intuition are still heightened under the full moon, and especially creativity, as Aries & Libra both amp up creative energy.

Place mugwort, lavender, witch hazel blossoms & catnip in a purple-colored sachet to make a talisman for divination and prophetic dreams. Any divination spells concerning love vibe particularly well with these herbs, and Libra is great for insight into relationships.

Try to incorporate the element of air into rituals & spellwork, as it is Libra's element. Wands & blades can both be used to represent the element of air as well, making this a good time to bless those ritual tools or charge them in the light of the moon. Or, if the weather is nice enough, go to a local park to collect wood to make a new wand. Remember to use only fallen wood & to thank the tree for its gift!

You can also try singing or chanting a spell. This can be amplified with many voices; air signs are symbolic of connection. Or release the pent-up energy of Aries season, and scream it out.

Witch's bells are also an excellent way to combine Libra's airy elemental energy with Aries' protective vibes. These bells are hung alongside a pentacle in sets of three or five. They are usually placed on the handle of doors as charms to ward away spirits and bad energy.

Remember too, that the chaotic, fickle nature of the element can work against your spells. It can help to try to keep a balance of the elements on your altar when casting. This can be accomplished with a single candle, as long as it is lit! The flame is the fire, the hard wax for the earth, air to feed the flame, and the melted wax for water.

Adding ingredients such as burdock burrs, or other local hitchhiker plants, and tacky plant resins to help your spells 'stick' under chaotic air signs.

Magick for the Libra Waning Gibbous Moon

The waning gibbous moon in Libra occurs from October to April. This means the sun will be in either Libra, Scorpio, Sagittarius, Capricorn, Aquarius, Pisces, Aries, or Taurus.

Your rituals & spells can be tailored to fit the energies of both celestial bodies. You can also consider the availability of seasonal ingredients to use in your spellwork & honor the turning of the wheel.

This phase is conducive to magick that repels, banishes & destroys things. You can use the entire waning cycle to work some big magick. Knock your life back into balance — the waning Libra moon is a good time to get rid of things keeping you from happiness.

Cast spells to settle disputes or stop injustice. Break barriers between lovers & banish obstacles for healthy partnerships, relationships, or marriages. Banish poor self-confidence & bad impressions. Confront change in your relationships. All are favored under the Libra waning moon.

However, for the few days after the full moon, energies can feel low & it can be hard to focus. Use the time to meditate or journal instead. This is a good time for problem-solving & finding solutions, so set aside time to give thought to your problems.

Simple, soothing crafts & projects that don't require too much attention to detail are excellent under the lazy energies of the waning gibbous. Projects that produce items that can be given as gifts are very appropriate for Libra as well.

Try a batch of confidence-boost lip balm for yourself & your circle. Here's how to make it:

- I tablespoon beeswax pellets
- I tablespoon shea butter
- I tablespoon coconut or jojoba oil
- I teaspoon raw honey
- 5 drops lavender essential oil
- 5 drops lavender essential oil

I. In a double boiler, melt & mix the beeswax, butter & oil.
2. Remove from heat & incorporate honey & essential oils while stirring counterclockwise to banish thoughts of inadequacy & self-doubt.
3. Fill your containers & let it set before use.

Magick for the Libra Last Quarter Moon

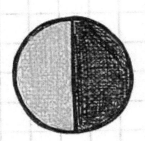

The last quarter moon in Libra occurs from October to April, meaning that the sun will be in either Libra, Scorpio, Sagittarius, Capricorn, Aquarius, Pisces, Aries, or Taurus at this time. The energies of both the sun & moon can be put to work magickally.

For instance, the energies of several of these signs aid in banishing roadblocks to creativity — Libra, of course, and also Aries, Taurus, Aquarius, Sagittarius & Pisces. Try burning orange and yellow candles if the sun is in a fire sign to do so. Or if the sun is in Taurus try using orange calcite crystals instead to take advantage of the elemental energies, while watery Pisces calls for a ritual bath!

Any obstacles for healthy partnerships, relationships, or marriages can also be banished under the waning Libra moon. It is a sign of cooperation & communication — Taurus & Aquarius vibe with this as well. And the waning moon is great at helping us to get rid of things we don't want.

Use the energy of Libra to help bring your life back into

balance & banish what's been blocking your path. Burn away obstacles by smoke cleansing with lemongrass, sage & some bay leaves. Or crush these herbs & use them to dress a black candle. Black is the color of banishing & protection, and burning a black candle before spellwork clears the space & protects your work from interference.

Libra also supercharges any spells involving air; use your breath or a feather to aid in any spell.

Knot magick especially vibes well with the element of air, and a witch's ladder can be customized & used for many magickal purposes, banishing, protection, manifesting, warding, etc.

To make, simply knot or braid a cord while focusing on a specific magickal intent. Incorporate pieces of paper with sigils or intentions written on them into the braid or chain of knots, as well as herbs, crystals, or symbolic items.

The nature of the items, the number of knots, and the color of the cord can vary with the intent.

Magick for the Libra Waning Crescent Moon

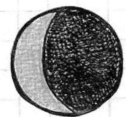

The waning crescent moon in Libra can occur from October to April. This means the sun will be in either Libra, Scorpio, Sagittarius, Capricorn, Aquarius, Pisces, Aries, or Taurus at this time. Channel the energy of both the sun & the moon into your spellwork & rituals.

For example, Aries helps banish obstacles to self-confidence, while Aquarius works well with Libra to be rid of blocks in communication. The waning crescent is a very powerful time for casting bigger banishing spells & releasing energies that aren't serving you.

Revenge spells are precisely the type of destructive magick the Libra moon likes. But beware of the energy rebounding. Libra will dole out justice where it sees fit and the chaotic nature of this air sign can be hard to direct.

Some witches abide by the threefold law, which says the energy that you send out into the universe will return back to you with 3 times the force. So take care with casting spells that intend to harm!

Libra gives also us an awareness of how other people see us. This is a good time to confront change in relationships & how we connect to each other. Use the waning moon's light to banish obstacles for healthy partnerships, relationships, or marriages. Taurus & Scorpio are good signs for the sun to be in for this work.

When writing spells, a feather quill pen is a valuable tool, especially under an air sign like Libra. Although finding the perfect feather can be difficult, it is incredibly rewarding.

The best feathers to use are about I0 inches long, and many feathers that fit this bill are from protected birds. Even the possession of these feathers can result in fines, so be careful. Geese or turkeys are great sources for feathers though, and so are crows! Here's how to make a quill pen:

I. Strip off the bottom bits of feather to form a grip for yourself — two inches or so. Scissors work well for this, but you'll need a small blade to scrape off the membrane from the tip of the feather. Do so gently!

2. On the underside of the feather's natural curve, cut into the shaft towards the tip at a sharp, steep slanted angle, so that the tip is cut in half. The remaining tip should be roughly triangular.

3. Remove the pith — the pulpy material inside the feather shaft — carefully, but completely.

4. Cut further to refine the tip of the pen. A pointy tip creates a fine line, while a broad, square tip is perfect for calligraphy.

5. Cut a ½ inch slit into the tip of the quill for the ink to flow. Or use your fingers to pinch the tip until one cracks naturally.

♏ Scorpio Magick

RULING PLANETS:

♂ ♀

Mars & Pluto

SPELLS FOR:

divination & dreaming
the dead & spirits
sex & intimacy
transformation
rebirth

WATER MAGICK: ▽

When the moon is in a
water sign, like Scorpio,
magick involving water
is quite powerful;
especially natural water
like the ocean or rain.

Water's elemental
direction is west

The element of water is
also associated with
cauldrons or chalices.

CRYSTALS:

jasper, ruby,
topaz, black opal,
smoky quartz,
labradorite, onyx,
obsidian &
bloodstone

HERBS:

sage,
foxglove,
mugwort,
coriander, basil,
rosemary, thistle,
yarrow, catnip & nettles

TAROT:
Death
king of cups
knight of wands
5,6,7 of cups

Magick for the Scorpio New Moon

The Scorpio new moon occurs with the sun in Scorpio, around the end of October & the beginning of November.

Think harvest & Samhain vibes — at least for the Northern Hemisphere. Remember in the Southern Hemisphere, it is the opposite time of year & around the Beltane season!

Part of the beauty of witchcraft is celebrating the cycles of the year, and certain rituals & spellwork just make sense at certain times of the year.

Brew up an apple cider with ginger & cinnamon to warm your soul as the nights get colder, as well as amp up your own magickal energy. And it's absolutely perfect for any autumn ritual. Make something magickal out of store-bought cider:

- I gallon cider; alcoholic or non
- 4 cinnamon sticks
- ¼ cup honey or sugar
- I peeled piece of ginger
- 2 cloves

I. Combine all ingredients to a crockpot and let sit for 2-4 hours. Or use a stockpot and let simmer on a stovetop.
2. For an extra kick, add 2 cups of bourbon or whiskey after brewing. Serve hot.

Apple cider can be used as a substitute for other alcohols in a ritual, or as a non-alcoholic option, as ciders come both spiked and not.

Mars, Scorpio's ruling planet in classic astrology, is the planet of aggression and empowers iron & the element of fire — explaining why Scorpio sometimes feels like fire coming out of the tap rather than water. It is fearless & forceful. As a water sign though, Scorpio naturally vibes with spells involving water. Using a cast-iron cauldron can be a perfect way to meld all of these elements; try charging your moon water in it!

Moon water charged during the dark of the moon is excellent for cleansings, fresh starts, intention setting, and also shadow work — something that is perfect with Scorpio's energy.

Scorpio's watery element means bath rituals are also an excellent idea! Bathing before a ritual cleanses the mind, body, and soul. It allows us to meditate and lets us wash away the mundane.

Before the start of any ritual, a basic bath for purification & protection can be drawn; some would say this should always be done. However, each bath can be tailored to your spell's intentions. Crystals, candles, essential oils, herbs, salts, glitter, or honey can all be implemented for a magical soak. Dyes can even be added for color correspondences. An entire ritual can be performed, submerged.

Try using any combination of bergamot, sage, mugwort, catnip, or lavender essential oils in a ritual bath to aid in lifting the veil & inducing visions. Ring your tub with crystals like sodalite, blue kyanite, or amethyst to encourage your intuition. Just take care as not all crystals are water-safe! Take a soak before a tarot or rune reading. The Scorpio new moon favors spellwork for divination or dreaming.

The Scorpio new moon is the ultimate rebirth. It has us looking hard at our fears & vulnerabilities. Spells involving transformation, shame, secrets, the hidden, the taboo, sex, intimacy, power & control vibe well with the sign.

Using Scorpio's transformative energies? Try performing your spell beneath a rowan's branches; the energy of rowan trees aid in spells for transitions & transformation. Rowan wood can also be used to make wands, amulets & more. Or try carving a sigil for change into the wood!

Water, Scorpio's element, can be easily employed in a transformation spell as well. On the night of the Scorpio new moon, write your intention on a scrap of paper, and put it in a small, freezer-safe cup or container filled with moon water. Then, put the container in your freezer, and let it sit until the full moon. During the night of the full moon, take your container out of the freezer. Let the water melt, and if possible evaporate as well. Burn or bury your scrap of paper.

Butterflies also make great ingredients in spell sachet or jar spells for transformation, but if you're not ready for change & creation at this time, then beware!

Magick for the Scorpio Waxing Crescent Moon

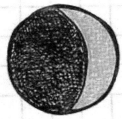

The waxing crescent moon in Scorpio occurs from May to November. This means the sun will be in either Taurus, Gemini, Cancer, Leo, Virgo, Libra, Scorpio, or Sagittarius. Use the energies of both the sun & the moon in your spellwork, or simply focus on the moon's.

For example, Taurus, Leo, or Libra work with Scorpio's sensual energies. Litter your altar with rose petals and red lipstick; they radiate love and readiness. Wear the lipstick and etch your beloved's name into a candle, and then burn it little by little every day leading up to the full moon.

Often associated with the darker aspects of life, Scorpio is compatible with most spellwork, but especially spellwork involving secrets, transformation, the spirits, death, rebirth, sex, intimacy & power; and the waxing phases are perfect for spells that pull our desires towards us.

Under a Scorpio moon, you can employ seashells to help keep a secret hidden. They have powerful protective energies & are representative of Scorpio's watery element as well. A found whelk, conch, or cowrie shell works the best for this, as they have a deeper chamber that can be sealed. Just make sure there are no creatures inside before you take it home. Then, make sure you are completely alone before whispering your secret into the shell & sealing it with black wax.

Embrace Scorpio's need for change & rebirth. Let go & transform. Try placing an inspiring tarot or oracle card to represent what you want to be or wish to attract to help direct those transformative energies. To take full advantage of Scorpio's transformative elements, cast your spells at sunset — during the transformation from day to night. If making moon water, set it out just before sunset to capture these powerful vibes.

Scorpio wants us to look at our vulnerabilities & to have us face our demons & dark side. Commit to trying to understand yourself a little better. Journal daily & smoke cleanse with mugwort & rosemary to unearth secrets as the moon waxes. Or rather than burning the herbs, try using essential oils & moon water in a diffuser!

You can also put moon water in a saucepan or kettle with herbs to diffuse their scent as well. Mixtures with citrus clear negativity, while cinnamon, honey & clove can calm & sweeten emotions at a time when emotional volatility can get in our way. Even to the point of causing spellwork to flounder.

Divination work also vibes well with the Scorpio moon. Break out your pendulum or tarot deck & seek out answers that have been eluding you.

Magick for the Scorpio First Quarter Moon

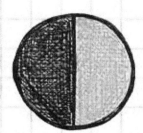

The first quarter moon in Scorpio occurs from May to November, meaning the sun will reside in either Taurus, Gemini, Cancer, Leo, Virgo, Libra, Scorpio, or Sagittarius. The energies of both the sun & moon can be put to work magickally.

Scorpio is compatible with most spellwork & the waxing moon has powerful energies for growth & to draw things to us. Use Scorpio's elemental energy to do so. As a water sign, Scorpio empowers any spell involving water; try a bath or brewing tea.

Try your hand at scrying with some moon-charged water. Silver bowls are supposed to work best, and prophecy, dreaming & divination come naturally under a Scorpio moon. The sun in Gemini or Scorpio adds to that energy.

Melted wax is also representative of water and can be used for scrying & divination. Paraffin & beeswax candles burn off almost completely, so soy candles are the best choice if you wish to read the way the wax drips as the candle burns. Clockwise & counterclockwise dripping patterns can mean your intent is moving closer or further from you.

But any candle's wax can be dripped into cold water in a scrying bowl. When reading wax this way, the melted wax is read as you would tea leaves.

Scorpio — ruled in part by Pluto the planet of death & darkness — also favors work with the spirit world & the dead. Use the strength of the waxing moon to summon a helpful spirit. Cast a circle of salt & sage for protection. A pentacle, especially one made from iron or silver, is a powerful protection tool & symbol of white magick. Wear one or place one on your altar while you work for protection!

Spells for intimacy, power & control are also all especially potent under a Scorpio moon, and the sun in Leo vibes with this too. Just remember to use caution & consent with any binding or manipulative magick.

Honey helps to summon love & lust, while thyme & lavender are aphrodisiacs; and they all can be added to a bath! Or use the power of touch & a few drops of lavender essential oils in a tablespoon of olive oil & give your partner a massage. Sex magick & orgasms can be powerful tools for manifesting!

Magick for the Scorpio Waxing Gibbous Moon

The waxing gibbous moon in Scorpio occurs from May to November. Therefore, the sun can reside in either Taurus, Gemini, Cancer, Leo, Virgo, Libra, Scorpio, or Sagittarius at this time. The energies of both celestial bodies can be put to work, and Scorpio is actually compatible with most spellwork, making it easier to coordinate spellwork with the sun's energies or seasonal vibes.

The waxing phases are perfect for spells that pull our desires towards us. Draw it in; use the moon's inward pull to your advantage. Stir your coffee clockwise, open your windows, hang your laundry to air out in the breeze. Do what you can to open your path to new energy & change.

Scorpio naturally vibes with spellwork & rituals involving the element of water. Bath rituals are also a great choice with the moon in Scorpio. Bathe in lavender & rose petals to summon up sex & love with the energy of the waxing moon.

Or try a mugwort & thyme bath to restore courage in the face of your vulnerabilities. The Scorpio moon is excellent for shadow work, but it can be intense. Mugwort, catnip & lavender can also be used in a pre-ritual bath to aid in inducing visions & cosmic connection.

And don't forget to leave some water to charge out in the moonlight. The lunar energy of the waxing moon imbues your moon water with the energy for growth, success, action & inspiration. You can use it later to bless a magickal bath or to brew up coffee or tea. Just make sure you are using clean water & storing it properly if you intend to digest it!

Scorpio's energy also especially energizes divination. Reading runes or doing a tarot spread are perfect activities.

However, suspicion & volatile emotions can cause spellwork to flounder under this sign. Take time to ground yourself & affirm your relationships, especially if things feel clouded. While Scorpio has us focused on the spirit, it is important to not forget the physical entirely.

Magick for the Scorpio Full Moon

The Scorpio full moon occurs with the sun in Taurus, around the end of April & the beginning of May.

The Taurus season spans from April to May, this means the Scorpio full moon only occurs during one of these two months. If it is April, then the moon is considered the Pink Moon, but in May it is known as the Flower Moon.

In the Northern Hemisphere, this is the season of Beltane. Fresh flowers, like daisies, can be used as altar decorations or offerings this time of year. Daisy chains, wreaths, or crowns, which bring luck & love when worn, can be incorporated into rituals as well — the flower vibes well with Taurus' energies.

To create a simple daisy chain, collect flowers with similar stem lengths and clean off leaves & greenery from the stems. Then, using your fingernail, puncture the bottom of the stem to create a small slit. Another flower can then be fed through the slit, like a buttonhole, to the flower head. This step can be repeated until you have the length you desire. Then, connect your first & last daisies to form a circle! Daisy stems are fairly flexible and can be braided to form a thicker band of flowers as well.

Remember in the Southern Hemisphere, it is the opposite time of year & the season of Samhain. Either way, emotions & intuition are usually heightened during the full moon, especially when the veil is thin in the days preceding the sabbats, and the Scorpio full moon can be particularly emotionally intense.

Scorpio likes to have us confront our demons & dark side — think shadow work. Anything involving shame, secrets, the hidden, or the taboo. Be aware that emotional volatility can cause spellwork to flounder.

Scorpio has extremely powerful transformative energies, and hag stones are a great way to combine the earthen energy of Taurus with Scorpio's.

Hag stones are stones with natural holes in them, which are caused by water erosion — although boring mollusks can also cause them — over thousands of years. This infuses these stones with the power of transformation & deep subterranean waters. While they are perfect for transformative jar or sachet spells, they can also be used in spellwork for fertility, for warding away bad dreams, or to see into other realms or the future by looking through the hole.

Scorpio is also a great sign for divination; particularly concerning life changes, inner desires & personal growth.

Charge divination tools in the moonlight, as well as moon water. The full moon gives us the most powerful lunar energy in the moon's cycle, and can imbue your water with those energies for later spellwork. As a water sign, Scorpio naturally vibes with any spell involving water. This element is the most in sync with the moon!

Mugwort in particular aids in calling down dreams. It can be smoked or made into tea. Or add rose petals & honeysuckle to a mugwort bath for erotic dreaming. Spells for love, sex & intimacy are very potent under both Scorpio & Taurus.

Honey is used for binding spells, spells involving love and lust, bringing people together, and 'sweetening' attitudes in general. Lavender, which works well with Scorpio, can be used to encourage love & pleasant feelings. Lavender honey is particularly potent for magical use. To create a honey jar binding spell:

I. Push a slip of paper into a jar of honey along with a sprig of lavender and 3 basil leaves. On that slip of paper write the name of the person you wish to bind to yourself.
2. Lick your fingers clean and visualize the person.

Remember to use caution when casting love or binding spells, as they are strong magic and can be harmful & manipulative.

Magick for the Scorpio Waning Gibbous Moon

The waning gibbous moon in Scorpio occurs from November to May. This means the sun will reside in either Sagittarius, Capricorn, Aquarius, Pisces, Aries, Taurus, or Gemini.

Consider how you can incorporate the energies of both the sun & the moon into your work. Scorpio is actually compatible with most spellwork, so it can be easy to coordinate spellwork with the signs of both celestial bodies.

The waning phases are perfect for magick that repels, banishes & destroys things, pushing away what we do not want. You can use the entire waning cycle to work some big magick. Let go of obsessions, past lovers, jealousy & secrets during the waning Scorpio moon. Scorpio likes shadow work — shame, secrets & the hidden. Write down what you wish to change about yourself. Bind it with black thread & burn. Work towards manifesting that reality.

Remember that for the few days after the full moon, energies can feel sapped & slow as the moon recedes, making it a good time to rest & relax.

Or tap into the mystical vibes that Scorpio brings; it's a good sign for divination, particularly with life changes desires & growth. Consult tarot deck or runes. Start a journal. Often our subconscious already knows the answer we don't want to see.

This is also a good moon phase for cleansings. As a water sign, baths & showers are extra refreshing & magickally charged under Scorpio. Try a bath bomb or a shower steamer with essential oils & dried herbs. Both are simple to make, but shower steamers are definitely the easier of the two for the busy witch! Here's how to make them:

- I cup baking soda
- ½ cup citric acid
- ¼ cup cornstarch
- 20-30 drops of essential oils
- Spray bottle of witch hazel
- Dried herbs, optional

I. Combine baking soda, citric acid, dried herbs, cornstarch & essential oils in a bowl.
2. Spray your dry mixture slowly with witch hazel while mixing. Continue until the mixture has the consistency of wet sand. It should clump & hold its shape when squeezed.
3. Press the mixture gently into molds — muffin pans work well — and allow to dry

To use, just bring one into the shower & let the water do its work! They are best placed lightly out of a direct shower spray. Store in an airtight container.

Magick for the Scorpio Last Quarter Moon

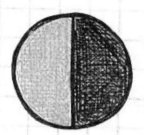

The last quarter moon in Scorpio can occur from November to May. This means the sun will reside under Sagittarius, Capricorn, Aquarius, Pisces, Aries, Taurus, or Gemini. The energies of both the sun & moon can be put to use when planning spellwork & rituals.

A hot herbal bath or a cup of tea can be a treat during the colder months of the year. Let the warmth of the water seep into your bones. As a water sign, Scorpio naturally vibes with the element's energy.

The waning phases are most conducive to magick that repels, banishes, or destroys. Let go of obsessions, past lovers, jealousy & secrets during the waning Scorpio moon. An easy way to use the element of water in your banishing spells is to write down what you wish was out of your life in chalk on your sidewalk, or any convenient concrete, just before a storm, and let the rainwater wash it out of your life. Or write those same intentions — gently! — on toilet paper & flush it!

And of course, water is the perfect element for cleansings as well. Mix a few drops of sage & frankincense essential oils with moon water in a spray bottle & spritz to cleanse your space. Or do a deeper cleaning and add a few drops of moon water to your mop bucket.

Remember to consider the time of day when casting too. Spells for divination are best done during the night, while banishings & cleansings do well at sunset — and all of this spellwork works well under Scorpio.

When doing a tarot reading or casting runes during the waning moon, look to the past for answers rather than straining to look ahead.

The Scorpio moon can be emotionally intense, which can work with & against your spellwork. Emotional volatility, anger & suspicion can cause spellwork to flounder, but this is also a good moon for shadow work. Take a look at your darker side & learn from it!

Magick for the Scorpio Waning Crescent Moon

The waning crescent moon in Scorpio can occur from November to May, meaning the sun will be in either Sagittarius, Capricorn, Aquarius, Pisces, Aries, Taurus, or Gemini at this time. You can tailor your spells to fit the energies of both celestial bodies & seasonal energies, and although those energies can vary quite a bit throughout the year, Scorpio is compatible with most spellwork.

However, the waning crescent is a powerful time for casting out anything you no longer want in your life. Be rid of stubborn spirits — Scorpio favors work with the spirit world — or let go of obsessions, jealousy, or secrets. Banish & burn them away with sage & bay.

Or symbolically suspend a person & their actions between two mirrors by writing their name on a scrap of paper and placing it between the two mirrors. Compact mirrors are excellent for this. The name can also be written directly onto the glass, and a photo or a lock of hair will work as well.

Mirrors, which are also symbolic of Scorpio's element, water, should always be cleansed before use in spellwork. This is especially true of mirrors bought second-hand!

Rosemary & black pepper, which are both associated with protection & banishment, can be infused into a potent simple syrup. The simple syrup can be mixed into lemonade or grapefruit juice to create a brew to banish just about anything. Here's how to make it:

- ½ cup water or moon water
- ½ cup sugar
- 2-3 sprigs of fresh rosemary
- I teaspoon coarsely ground pepper

1. Strip rosemary from stems & roughly chop. Discard stems.
2. Combine all ingredients in a small saucepan & bring to a boil, while stirring occasionally.
3. Remove from heat, allow to cool & strain.
4. Stir into your beverage of choice counterclockwise & sip to magickally charge yourself.

For an extra kick and if you're of age, spike with a shot of brandy or grapefruit vodka. Salt & pepper the rim of your glass for extra protection.

Water is the element of emotion & as a water sign, Scorpio vibes with the element's energy, which can leave us sometimes too tuned into our feelings. The raw emotional energy can get in the way of spellwork. But, if you can handle it, Scorpio is also good for working with intimacy & vulnerabilities.

As the moon fades, we are confronted with uncomfortable endings & the impermanent nature of things. Embrace it. Let go & transform.

Sagittarius Magick

RULING PLANET:
Jupiter ♃

FIRE MAGICK: △

Under a fire sign, like Sagittarius, the moon vibes well with magick involving fire, incense & candles.

Fire's elemental direction is south.

The element of fire is also associated with wands or ceremonial blades.

SPELLS FOR:
travel
creativity
truth & purpose
communication
connection
growth

HERBS:
mint, sage, rose, hyssop, lavender, borage, vervain, bay, feverfew, calendula, dandelion & clove

CRYSTALS:
amethyst, sodalite, turquoise, lapis lazuli, aventurine, topaz, amber, diamond & sapphire

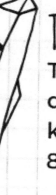

TAROT:
Temperance
queen of pentacles
knight of wands
8,9,10 of wands

Magick for the Sagittarius New Moon

The Sagittarius new moon occurs when the sun is also in Sagittarius, which is around the end of November & beginning of December. The new moon is the best time for new beginnings & Sagittarius absolutely loves new things.

The new moon is when you should set intentions for the upcoming lunar cycle. Visualize your goals & make a list of what you need to do to set your dreams in motion. As a fire sign, Sagittarius has marvelous transformative energy, so dream big! Tarot or oracle cards can be used as guidance.

With the double dose of Sagittarian energy, we can feel stifled. Use the new moon to plan a trip or vacation. Order a new book on a subject you've always wanted to know more about or sign up for a class!

Jupiter, which rules Sagittarius, promotes growth. It is a planet of optimism & expansiveness, but it is also easy to lose yourself in those energies. It is a good idea to perform a grounding ritual before working with them.

And although Sagittarius's energy is generally uplifting & positive, when the moon is truly dark in the sky, it's better to rest, performing only limited spellwork. This is a good time for journaling & other low-energy creative projects. Fire signs grant us creative energy & the element vibes with the spontaneous. Remember to consider the color ink you use when journaling or planning. Blue amps up creative energy, while purple sparks the imagination.

As Sagittarius is a sign of communication, consider writing a letter to a friend or relative — without actually mailing it. After writing, send the intentions you wrote cosmically by burning the letter under the dark moon.

Tap into Sagittarius' elemental energy by working with candle magick. Dress your candle in oil & herbs that correspond to your spell's intent.

This extra step in your ritual gives you a chance to further imbue your working with your energy. Oil helps the herbs stick. Grind down your herbs finely & roll the oiled candle in them, while visualizing your outcome. Just be careful when lighting, as the herbs are flammable and can cause the entire candle to turn into a torch!

Tarot or rune readings and divination of all sorts work well under this moon. Sagittarius helps us to connect with the higher powers & find meaning in the world.

Amethysts bridge this world to the divine, while topaz channels divine energy & aids in manifestation — use either as a pendulum or just set them out while you work! Or draw down dreams by smoke cleansing with sage, mugwort & catnip.

With candle magick empowered under Sagittarius, it is a perfect time to try reading candle wax. Fill your scrying bowl with cool moon water and light a candle. Try picking a color that vibes with your intent. Then, with a question in your mind, hold the candle carefully over the bowl & let the wax drip into the water. Snuff out your candle and meditate on what you see in the drippings.

Fire's elemental energy is best put to use when you are seeking rapid results from your spellwork, but not long-lasting ones. Fast & unpredictable, it has a tendency to harm as well as help. You can use the other elements to help balance this out though. Employ water & earth into your spellwork to soothe & slow the burn of fire.

Conversely, you can lean into fire's urgency to burn. Coffee vibes well with that fiery Sagittarian energy. It's a great power boost for nearly any spell; use any time your spells need to produce results immediately. Use the beans or sprinkle ground coffee into spell sachets & jars. Or draw sigils in your morning brew and sip.

Magick for the Sagittarius Waxing Crescent Moon

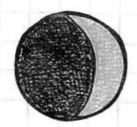

The waxing crescent moon in Sagittarius occurs from June to December. This means the sun will be in either Gemini, Cancer, Leo, Virgo, Libra, Scorpio, Sagittarius, or Capricorn. Your spellwork can be made to suit both signs, as well as seasonal energies, of course.

For example, Gemini & Leo vibe well with any spells for creativity, while Scorpio is a perfect pairing for divination & dreamwork. Listen to Sagittarius moon's call to connect with your tribe & sit down for a group reading.

Sagittarius is a sign that thrives on the new & unknown. Try casting a new spell or working with a crystal you've never used before. Or leave an offering to an unfamiliar deity. Sagittarius is a great time to connect with the higher powers.

Harness the sign's super-charged firepower & need for the novel by burning a new incense or by making your own! Your own handcrafted incense is a powerful tool to use for future rituals for many moons to come, and it can be made with any combination of your favorite herbs. Pick an herb you've never

worked with before to further explore Sagittarius's curiosity.
Here is an easy recipe for incense cones:

- 3 teaspoons ground herbs
- I teaspoon makko powder

I. If your herbs are not already ground, use a mortar &
   pestle or coffee grinder to grind them finely.
2. Mix the ground herbs & makko powder until all ingredients
   are evenly distributed.
3. Add water 5-I0 drops at a time to the mixture until it
   reaches a dough-like consistency, easily moldable by hand.
4. Form your cones by hand or use a mold.
5. Let dry for I2-48 hours. This will depend on the humidity
   in your area.

Light your incense cone from the tip & enjoy!

Or tap into Sagittarius's penchant for travel & cast a travel
protection spell. Paint sigils on the soles of your shoes. Or
carve a charm from a comfrey root & let it charge in the
moonlight.

And even though Sagittarius's energy is usually positive,
arrogance or a know-it-all attitude can cause spellwork to
flounder under a Sagittarius moon.

Magick for the Sagittarius First Quarter Moon

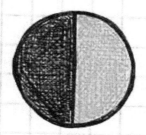

The first quarter moon in Sagittarius occurs from June to December. This means that the sun will reside under either Gemini, Cancer, Leo, Virgo, Libra, Scorpio, Sagittarius, or Capricorn at this time. The energies of both celestial bodies & their signs can be incorporated into your work, or you can choose to work with only the moon's energies.

For instance, Scorpio & Sagittarius make a wonderful pairing for spells to inspire change & personal transformation. Fire, Sagittarius' element, cannot exist without first consuming something, and therefore represents transformation — think phoenix mythology!

During the waxing moon, spells for growth & pulling our desires towards us are empowered. So, cast a glamour spell to boost self-confidence. Change up your hair, clothes, or makeup — do something drastically different from your norm!

Anoint your mirror with rose oil to help yourself & others see the sweeter things first. Use moon water to wash your hair or face. Or burn a candle anointed with sage & mint to help clear the air during your morning routine. The sun in Leo or Libra can amp up these energies too!

The moon under Sagittarius is also an excellent time to look for truth & meaning in the world. The element of fire also represents clarity & enlightenment.

So, let Sagittarius help you bring the truth to light. Fill a jar or sachet with herbs to help find the truth, like bay, calendula, marjoram & sunflower petals. Write down the question you want answers to & add that as well. Aquamarine is a great gem to add, as it is said to find hidden truths & inspire trust.

This is also a good sign for divination, like tarot or rune readings. Cast a circle of salt for protection before smoke cleansing with mugwort & sage to call down the unknown.

Sagittarius wants us to see growth just as much as experience it. Light blue & green candles for — communication & growth — and invite your circle over.

Group spellwork also vibes with Sagittarius, so it's a great time to have your coven come together! Have everyone bring a separate ingredient to cook a meal, or choose a different herb that represents them to combine for a group incense & burn in a ritual together.

Magick for the Sagittarius Waxing Gibbous Moon

The waxing gibbous moon in Sagittarius can occur from June to December, which means that the sun will be under either Gemini, Cancer, Leo, Virgo, Libra, Scorpio, Sagittarius, or Capricorn. Coordinate your spellwork with the sun's energies or even the seasons.

The sun in Gemini, Leo, or Sagittarius amplifies the Sagittarius moon's creative energies. Set aside time for creative projects: dance, paint, write poetry, or break in a new coloring book!

Amp up those energies even more with new crystals. Amber stimulates self-expression & creativity, and it vibes well with Sagittarius' energy. Or light a few candles to change the aura in your room to something more inspiring! Fire's energy is intensely creative!

If you enjoy using seasonal shiz in your spells & the time of year allows for it, try meditating in a field with plenty of dandelions. The flowers invite the expansiveness of the universe into our minds — perfect for Sagittarius's vibes.

Or if the weather is cooling, take advantage of Sagittarius's social vibes with a gathering of your circle around a fire & pot of hot mulled wine. Here's how to make it:

- I bottle of merlot or zinfindel
- ¼ cup cinnamon whiskey
- I-3 tablespoons of honey
- 3 whole star anise
- 2 whole cinnamon sticks
- 6 whole cloves
- I large orange, peeled & sliced into rounds

I. Combine all the ingredients in a saucepan or crockpot.
2. Cook on low to medium heat. Keep covered & stir occasionally for I5 minutes to up to 3 hours. You can serve it hot, straight from the stovetop.

Star anise brings clairvoyance & luck — both vibe with Sagittarius — and cinnamon & clove are connected to the element of fire, making this the perfect brew for a chilly Sagittarian moon!

Take Sagittarius's wanderlust & put it to use by checking out new scenery. Even if you don't go very far. A different country or a new park, it doesn't matter. The Sagittarius moon has us seeking the world outside ourselves. Sagittarius delights in the new — tools, toys, knowledge, friends. Explore a shop, take a class, or invite someone for coffee. These fiery vibes won't last forever! Or try a new way to connect to the unknown; a new set of runes, a crystal pendulum, tea leaves, etc.

And while Sagittarius is a quite confident sign, a know-it-all attitude or arrogance can cause spellwork to falter under a Sagittarius moon.

Magick for the Sagittarius Full Moon

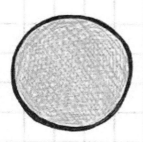

The Sagittarius full moon occurs with the sun in Gemini — around the end of May & the beginning of June — near the height of summer in the Northern Hemisphere, just before Midsummer.

The Gemini season spans from May to June, this means the Sagittarius full moon only occurs during one of these two months. If it is May, the moon is known as the Flower Moon, but in June it is known as the Strawberry Moon.

This makes it a fantastic time for wildcrafting or harvesting summer herbs for your spellwork, as well as using them for decor for your altar & sacred spaces. Or take advantage of the warm weather & hold your rituals outdoors.

Holding a bonfire vibes with Sagittarius's call to connect with our tribe & the sign's elemental energy! Burn herbs & gaze into the flames. For fire signs, magick involving fire is quite powerful & the full moon heightens our intuition.

Use the full moon's energy to help you train & tap into your own intuition — or claircognizance — especially with Sagittarius pushing us to find our truth. From a tarot deck, separate the Moon major arcana & two other random cards. Keep them face down & shuffle. Spread them out & inspect; look, touch, listen. See if you can find the Moon.

You can also bring water, crystals & other magickal tools to charge in the moonlight. The full moon gives us the most powerful energy in the moon's cycle, imbuing items with that all-purpose lunar energy.

Emotions & intuition are heightened during the full moon, making this an excellent time to break out your tarot cards & seek out answers. Sagittarius wants to bring truth to light.

Buy a notebook just to take notes on your tarot spreads! You can put the date under them & analyze them at a later time. Or try a group ritual or a group tarot reading — Sagittarius likes us to connect with people.

This full moon gives us an opportunity to soul search and redefine what we believe in. Smoking herbs, like mugwort, cannabis, mullein, passionflower & more, can open your mind. Use with respect & caution, and only in appropriate doses!

This is also a great day to hold or attend a class & learn something new! The transfer of knowledge & skills is heightened under the Sagittarius full moon, a sign that loves to both collect & share information.

Or invite over your fellow witches & host an ingredient swap. Trade for something you've never worked with before or experiment with a new spell; Sagittarius likes the new & non-conforming.

In fact, new people & new places vibe hard with the

Sagittarian need for the novel. And the full moon can give us the courage we made need to leave our bubble and take that first step into something new. Burn brightly! This fiery energy won't last forever.

Fire & air signs are interchangeably associated with wands & ceremonial blades, which are also known as athame. Both of which can be used to draw circles of protection for spellwork & meditation. If you don't have these tools, this is a perfect time to find or make them, as Sagittarius delights in the new. Traditionally, a ceremonial blade is black- or white-handled, as well as double-edged. What is more important is that you choose a blade that vibes with you.

Or get crafty and try your hand at making your own wand — a personal & meditative experience. Select a stick that speaks to you & decorate. Crystals & herbs are easily glued or tied on, and twine or wire can be used to wrap a handle. You can also paint or carve the wood using colors, runes, or sigils that are important to you. Glitter, feathers, cloth, or charms can also be used.

With the moon in a fire sign & the sun in an air sign, this is a perfect full moon to anoint, bless, or charge your new wand or athame.

Magick for the Sagittarius Waning Gibbous Moon

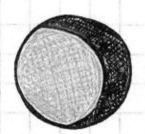

The waning gibbous moon in Sagittarius occurs from December to June. This means, during this time, that the sun can be in either Sagittarius, Capricorn, Aquarius, Pisces, Aries, Taurus, Gemini, or Cancer.

The waning phases are best for magick that repels, banishes & destroys what we do not want & need in our lives. You can use the entire waning cycle to work some big magick.

However, for the few days after the full moon, energies can feel sapped & slow as the moon recedes. And coffee is a great solution; it vibes well with Sagittarius too! Using moon water to brew your morning coffee can help give you an extra boost! Just make sure you are using clean water from a sanitized jar! Stir counterclockwise to banish tiredness & sip.

Remember that rituals & spells can be tailored to the seasons — as well as the energies of both the sun & the moon, and the signs they are under. Capricorn works with Sagittarius to banish the fear of failure & impediments to long-term goals.

Aquarius or Gemini help Sagittarius to break down barriers stopping you from connecting with others or communicating clearly; it's also an excellent combo for creative projects, divination of all sorts, or learning something new.

Sagittarius lets us radically rethink the world around us & what we believe in. Try experimenting with a new spell. Or go out and explore. The Sagittarius moon has us seeking the world outside ourselves

Harness the firepower of Sagittarius by smoke cleansing. Try wrapping your own herbal wand/smudge stick — it's pretty simple. Start by tying the stems of your herbs together and wrapping tightly downwards; preferably using natural, undyed cordage, so it burns cleanly.

Once you reach the end, wrap back toward the other end. Criss-cross your string as you wrap back the other way and tie it off at the end. You can also slip the new smudge stick into the oven at 170 F for an hour or so to speed up drying times.

Use sage & lavender for enlightenment or thyme & bay leaves for minor banishings. Garden sage is a perfect substitution for white sage in modern spellwork.

Remember that Sagittarius' energy can be very confident, yet that confidence can warp into arrogance & mess with the results of spellwork.

Magick for the Sagittarius Last Quarter Moon

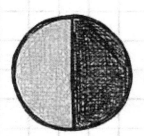

The last quarter moon in Sagittarius can occur from December to June, which means the sun can be under either Sagittarius, Capricorn, Aquarius, Pisces, Aries, Taurus, Gemini, or Cancer. You can sync up your spellwork & rituals to fit the energies of both the sun & moon, as well as seasonal energies.

The waning moon is an especially powerful time for banishings. Aquarius or Gemini work well with Sagittarius to be rid of blocks in creativity or communication, while Capricorn & Sagittarius work well in getting rid of impediments to long-term goals or the fear of failure. And Cancer & Sagittarius are a great pair for a cord-cutting ritual if you're looking to banish a particular person.

Cement your banishing by burning a black candle — remember Sagittarius amps up candle magick — to clear the way for your spellwork before starting. It can negate bad vibes & pave a smoother path to success.

Or make an offering to a deity & ask for their aid in the banishing. Sagittarius is an excellent sign for work with the higher powers. If you don't have a usual deity you work with, Sagittarius is a great sign to respectfully try working with a new one.

This is also a good time for group work as well as banishings. So band together with your coven to cast out bad energy by lighting a bonfire & tossing in herbs like sage, mugwort, rosemary, or bay leaves. Take turns writing down the things you wish to remove from your lives and throw them into the fire. If you are comfortable doing so, say it out loud as well. Then, sing, cheer & celebrate with your coven while the fire burns.

Fire magick is charged under fire signs like Sagittarius. This is especially so when the sun's strength is also growing in power, or major fire festivals like Beltane & Imbolc occur.

Based in Beltane traditions, it is also possible to purify yourself by passing between two flames. Try using two black candles near the doorway to your home or room to purify all who enter & leave, including you!

This is also a good time to experiment with a new spell, new people & new places.

Magick for the Sagittarius Waning Crescent Moon

The waning crescent moon in Sagittarius occurs from December to June, meaning that the sun can be in Sagittarius, Capricorn, Aquarius, Pisces, Aries, Taurus, Gemini, or Cancer.

Remember you can tailor your rituals & spellwork to fit the energies of both celestial bodies, and don't forget to take the time of year into account when decorating your altar or choosing spell ingredients.

For example, Aries, Aquarius, or Gemini work well with Sagittarius' creative energy. Use the waning moon to banish blocks in creativity, while Capricorn & Sagittarius work together better to banish the fear of failure, distractions, or impediments to long-term goals.

Try grabbing some St. John's wort & lavender to burn & banish anything that's bumming you out. Sagittarius generally brings positive vibes & good energy, and both herbs do too!

And the waning crescent is a powerful time for bigger banishings & casting out anything you no longer want in your life. This close to the dark moon is when those energies are at their strongest, so make sure to put them to work!

Both fire & blades, which are representative of the element, are excellent tools to use for severing ties & banishing spells. Fire burns things away & blades can be used to metaphorically cut things out of our lives.

Spellwork involving fire is particularly potent under fire signs like Sagittarius, so try to incorporate candles or another form of flame into your works. Fire's elemental energy is best put to use when you are seeking rapid results from your spellwork, but not long-lasting ones.

The waning crescent is also a great time for cleansings, and fire can be employed in purifications as well. Cleanse your blades, or other fire-safe tools by running them through a white candle's flame.

The Sagittarius moon is also a great time for divination, group work, truth spells, connecting with a new deity, or learning something new!

♑ Capricorn Magick

RULING PLANET: Saturn ♄

SPELLS FOR:
career success
planning & organizing
stability & structure
grounding

TAROT:
the Devil
king of swords
queen of pentacles
2,3,4 of pentacles

EARTH MAGICK: ▽

When the moon resides under an earth sign, like Capricorn, magick involving crystals, stones, salt, dirt, or roots is quite effective.

Earth's elemental direction is north.

The element of earth is also associated with pentacles & besoms.

HERBS:
sunflower, star anise,
chamomile, lemon balm,
basil, marjoram, thyme,
rosemary & yarrow

CRYSTALS:
onyx, garnet, obsidian,
smoky quartz, hematite,
jet & diamond

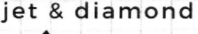

Magick for the Capricorn New Moon

The new moon in Capricorn occurs with the sun in Capricorn as well — around the end of December & the beginning of January. This means in the Northern Hemisphere that it is just around the season for Yule & Midwinter, while in the Southern it is the season for Midsummer.

If you enjoy using seasonal ingredients for offerings, decor, or in your spellwork, holly, mistletoe & pine go hand in hand with winter & the Yule season. All three are traditionally used in rituals, spellwork & celebrations this time of year. Holly & mistletoe should be treated with care, especially around pets & children, as they are both poisonous!

These plants are traditional symbols of immortality & rebirth. All three are commonly used as decor. Wreaths or garlands can be made from live greens. Spritz them with water to keep them fresh, and add essential oils to strengthen their scent as time passes.

Oak can also be included in spellwork or decor for either solstice, as there is folklore that associates both oak &

holly as kings that personify Yule & Midsummer.

When the moon is truly dark in the sky, it is best to refrain from major spellwork. It is a much better time to prepare for the upcoming lunar cycle & Capricorn loves to plan! Some of the best spellwork for the dark moon focuses on introspection & reflection, including self-growth. Capricorn, and its ruling planet, Saturn, give us a sense of structure & discipline. This new moon vibes especially well with manifesting goals in your career & finances. Organize & set goals.

Don't forget Capricorn is a wonderful sign for grounding & centering rituals too! Staying present & in control is essential with the moon in Capricorn. Work a ground ritual into your routine. Sit in the grass while you drink your coffee. Touch the soles of your feet to dirt, your palms, or even to lay down on the ground to feel the pulse of the earth. Place your head in the roots of a tree.

If you can't get outside hold your favorite crystal & focus your energy on it. Using grounding scents like vetiver & cedarwood in your home or office can also be helpful.

Capricorn's tendencies to focus on fear, sadness & negativity can cause spellwork to flounder. However, it is also an excellent sign for shedding that negative energy. Saturn, Capricorn's ruling planet, is associated with endings; perfect for banishing things from your life & establishing boundaries.

Try your hand at making black salt. This is a perfect moon for it! You can use it in your banishing & hex-break spells; it's particularly good for driving away negative energy. Sprinkle it around your property to keep your home safe or in the footprints of someone to make them go away.

A simple recipe for black salt is 2 parts sea salt, and I part ritual ashes, cauldron scrapings, or charcoal. Black pepper can also be added, as it grants protection & absorbs negativity too! Crush & mix the ingredients together with mortar & pestle. Charge under the dark moon. Then, store in an airtight container for later use.

Of course, this isn't the only time you can make black salt, but it is a good time for it considering the energies that are available. After burning your Yule greens at Imbolc is another powerful time to make it as well.

As an earth sign, Capricorn amps up the elemental energy of salt & earth as well. Also, consider working with dirt, roots, crystals, or clay too. Make your own runes with air-dry or oven-baked clay. It can be nice to have a few sets as they are perfect for adding to sachet & jar spells! If using air-dry clay, you can even press dried herbs into the surface for extra potency.

And although the new moon is usually a good time for such things, divination should be avoided under a Capricorn moon, as it is not a great sign for it. Capricorn much prefers work in the material work rather than the spiritual.

Magick for the Capricorn Waxing Crescent Moon

The waxing crescent moon in Capricorn can occur from July to January. This means the sun can reside in Cancer, Leo, Virgo, Libra, Scorpio, Sagittarius, Capricorn, or Aquarius. Spellwork can be tailored to fit the energies of both celestial bodies.

For example, a Capricorn moon with the sun in either Leo, Virgo, or Sagittarius gives us the energy to get things done. The moon grows in strength, and so do you! All three of these signs vibe ith career success, especially in creative fields. Put stones like black obsidian on your desk to absorb bad energy & redirect hate. Just remember to cleanse the crystal regularly, so that it can keep doing its job!

The sun in either Virgo & Capricorn in particular works with the pull of the waxing Capricorn moon to grant material & monetary success. Use the entire waxing phase; light a green candle carved with sigils reinforcing your intent — this can be as simple as using dollar signs!

Or make some 'rich witch' water by adding mint & lemon slices to your moon water. Stir clockwise & visualize money flowing into your life. You can also add or swap in any other edible money-drawing herbs you might prefer.

Keeping jade or citrine in your pocket can also attract wealth, especially as magick involving the element of earth is potent right now.

You can also put that earthen energy to work by burying your crystals — only those that won't be damaged by the elements — to charge & cleanse in the earth during the waxing moonlight. Or work with tree roots, crystals, dirt & other earthy magick to tap into that energy.

Seasonal energies & spell ingredients can be considered when casting as well. The Capricorn waxing moon can occur multiple times from summer to winter. Many bulb plants become available in the fall & winter, and there's a good chance the Capricorn waxing moon will fall near a good time to plant one. Write your intention for success down on paper and plant it with your bulb. With the proper care, you will watch your flowers & accomplishments grow with the waxing moon.

The Capricorn waxing moon calls for pragmatic, practical & purposeful steps towards our goals. Saturn, Capricorn's ruling planet, aids in spells for stability & success. And the sign's earthen energy aids in spellwork meant to work over a longer period of time. Use the energy to make plans, organize & set goals. Manifest a reality that makes you happy. But don't make plans if you can't put in the work!

It is also a good time for centering & grounding rituals.

Magick for the Capricorn First Quarter Moon

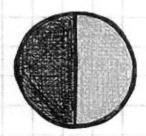

The first quarter moon in Capricorn can occur from July to January, which means the sun can be in either Cancer, Leo, Virgo, Libra, Scorpio, Sagittarius, Capricorn, or Aquarius. The energies of both signs should be considered when casting.

Virgo vibes well with Capricorn's career-driven nature, helping us draw in wealth & success, while Leo, Aquarius, or Libra can help Capricorn focus on our creative passions when planning for the future.

The waxing moon is perfect for pulling our desires towards us, and the Capricorn moon calls for pragmatic & purposeful steps towards our goals. It is a good time to take action — nothing is impossible with enough determination & hard work.

The Capricorn first quarter moon has strong energies & serious adult vibes to help summon structure & stability. Sage, vetiver & cedarwood are all grounding scents. Diffuse them, burn them, or put them in a scent sachet by placing these herbs in a drawstring bag along with cotton balls dabbed with the essential oils. The sachet is perfect for tucking into a clothing or desk drawer. It can also be placed in your car; hang it from your rearview mirror or tuck it under a seat!

In fact, it is an excellent time for centering & grounding rituals. Cast a circle with crystals. Ring yourself with them & pull their energies inward. Yarrow also offers powerful grounding and protective energy. Patches of yarrow, especially when found in the wild, indicate a spot of grounded energy. These patches make excellent places to meditate.

The waxing moon under Capricorn is also a good time for rituals to overcome negative influences, break boundaries, grow, and push ourselves onward. Doubly so if the sun is in a sign like Virgo or Sagittarius.

Brew up lemon balm tea to calm anxiety & bring on sleep because sometimes you need a break from the drive of Capricorn's energy. The plant grants strength & improves your mood, which is sometimes necessary as Capricorn can bring melancholy energy.

Magick for the Capricorn Waxing Gibbous Moon

The waxing gibbous moon in Capricorn can occur from July to January. This means the sun will be in either Cancer, Leo, Virgo, Libra, Scorpio, Sagittarius, Capricorn, or Aquarius at this time. The waxing gibbous moon is the last stage before the full moon & when we must trust that the intentions we set will come to fruition.

The waxing moon is best used for constructive magick; spells that pull our desires towards us. Just remember, during the gibbous phase, there is little time to harness that energy before the full moon. We can take the last steps we need to reach our goals & manifest our intentions.

Any newly cast spells should require little turnaround time. Use coffee grounds in your spellwork to speed them up, or a dab of oil to metaphorically grease the wheels. Remember earthy energy like Capricorn can be slow to start, but produces long-term results.

With the waxing moon in an earth sign, it is an excellent time to cast spells for material gain. Keep a magnet or lodestone in a change jar near the front door of your home to pull wealth in the door. Or try filling a small green or gold pouch with rice & keeping it on your person to attract luck & fortune. Rice has strong associations with luck & riches. It is also easily dyed green with food coloring to further tailor it to this cause.

Tap into those earthy energies further by carrying a crystal in your pocket or collecting stones for spellwork. Try molding clay into sigils or drawing them out with salt.

The Capricorn moon is a good time for centering & grounding rituals. Lay your head in the roots of your favorite tree. Let it empower you & ground you. Meditate. Recharge your energy.

The Capricorn waxing moon is also a good time to overcome negative influences, break boundaries, and grow. It is time to examine if our habits and influences are healthy for us. Visualize the future and make a list of what you want & don't want in it. Prepare to banish whatever is holding us back in the coming waning cycle.

Write a sigil or rune on your wrist for persistence to remind yourself of your commitment when trying to break a bad habit. Willpower & determination can be necessary.

Be aware that sadness, depression, trepidation & fear of failure is common under the Capricorn moon; to the point that spellwork can falter.

Magick for the Capricorn Full Moon

The full moon in Capricorn occurs with the sun in Cancer. As the Cancer season spans from June to July, this means the Capricorn full moon only occurs during these two months. If it is June the moon is the Strawberry Moon, but in July it is called the Buck Moon.

With the earth caught between the sun & the moon, we have the most powerful lunar energy in the moon's cycle. Divination comes naturally at the full moon, but under Capricorn, this work is best avoided. Yet emotions are still heightened at this time.

While Capricorn finds stability in physical accomplishments & career success, Cancer is fulfilled by emotional comfort & the spiritual. This seemingly dissonant full moon isn't about choosing one or the other. Both energies must be balanced.

Capricorn is ruled by Saturn, which represents coming of age, practicality & structure — very serious vibes! Saturn teaches us the discipline to go after our goals and to hold ourselves accountable. Nothing is impossible with enough hard work.

And while it is a great time to work on ourselves, it is also a great time to appreciate how far we've come. Celebrate all of your achievements, but also plan for those in the future. Consider leaving out offerings to the higher powers as thanks for your success. And don't forget to reward yourself as well!

The Capricorn moon is also a good time for centering & grounding rituals. Try setting up a crystal grid with stones that vibe with that energy like smokey quartz, jasper, or obsidian.

Alfalfa is also a potent addition to grounding rituals. Mix the herb, dried & crushed, into mixes for protection circles. Or scatter the ashes of the plant after burning.

Because of their strong associations with the moon, sliced lemons are great to charge in moon water. They also vibe well with the Cancer season's energies. After your water is finished, you can fish out the slices & dry them in the oven for later use.

Lemons are excellent ingredients in spellwork to dispel the melancholy that Capricorn brings — which can interfere with your magick! Salt & earth magick are empowered under Capricorn, and mixing salt & lemon is also a great way to celebrate both the sun & the moon. This edible sun salt is powerful in spellwork & useful in the kitchen. Use it to cleanse a space, cast a circle, or draw down the sun. It can also flavor poultry, pork, or asparagus.

- I cup coarse sea salt
- 3 dried lemon slices
- I tablespoon dried ginger
- I tablespoon dried rosemary
- I tablespoon dried thyme

Finely chop the lemon & ginger. Then, combine all ingredients
& mix. Make your salt early in the day to chare in the light
of the afternoon sun as well as the moonlight, so that it is
charged with the energies of both. Store in a sealed jar. The
salt can be further ground before use with a mortar & pestle
or loaded into a clean, empty pepper mill.

Cancer gives this full moon potent cleansing energies, so put
them to work! Brooms & witches go way back, and they are
representative of the earthen element as well. Ritual besoms
can be reserved for altars & ritual spaces, but your regular
household broom can still be charged to sweep all of the
negativity in your home right out the front door. And mopping
your floors with a few drops of mint & sage essential oils
mixed into your cleaning liquid can keep the negativity out!

And don't forget to leave out your crystal collection, tarot
cards, or moon water to bathe in the light of the full moon.

Magick for the Capricorn Waning Gibbous Moon

The waning gibbous moon in Capricorn occurs from January to July, meaning that the sun will be in either Capricorn, Aquarius, Pisces, Aries, Taurus, Gemini, Cancer, or Leo. Remember to consider the energies of both celestial bodies in your spellwork!

This phase is conducive to magick that repels, banishes & destroys things, pushing away what we do not want. Separation rituals, cord-cutting & breakup spells are excellent under the cold Capricorn waning moon. You can use the entire waning cycle to work some big magick. However, for the few days after the full moon, energies can feel sapped & slow as the moon recedes, making it a good time for introspection.

The moon in Capricorn is a great time for banishing old fears as well. Be aware that sadness, depression, fear & fear of failure is common under the Capricorn moon; to the point that it can cause spellwork to falter.

But you can use the energy of the waning moon to banish the natural depression that Capricorn imbues us with. Try brewing a cup of St. John's wort tea. Or hold a ritual to overcome those negative influences. Lavender & lemon are naturally uplifting scents. Mix a few drops of essential oils with moon water in a spray bottle & spritz to banish those somber vibes.

This is a good time to focus & work on ourselves. Capricorn teaches us the discipline to go after our goals and how to hold ourselves accountable. The waning Capricorn moon is a good time to release an over-inflated ego or excessive reliance on the material world. Take time to examine your relationship with your accomplishments & career.

Capricorn is pragmatic; make a pros & cons list for bigger decisions. Be ready to let go of what is no longer serving you! It's not quitting; it's paving the way for a new beginning!

Use the entire cycle of the waning moon to remove obstacles for success in your career. Spend some time figuring out what you need to do to get ahead. Planning is one of Capricorn's biggest strengths, and its earth element energy lends itself to spellwork that takes time to grow & gather strength slowly. The element grants the endurance & stamina necessary for long-term success.

Capricorn is ruled by Saturn, a planet that represents structure, stability & groundedness, making this is a good time for centering & grounding rituals as well.

Magick for the Capricorn Last Quarter Moon

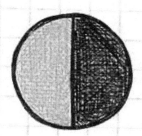

The last quarter moon in Capricorn can occur from January to July, meaning that the sun will reside under Capricorn, Aquarius, Pisces, Aries, Taurus, Gemini, Cancer, or Leo. And the energies of both those signs can be considered in spellwork as well.

For example, Taurus & Capricorn drive us to achieve monetary success. Smudge with protective & money-drawing herbs like basil, thyme & sage to destroy any obstacles on your path to success. The Capricorn last quarter moon is a particularly good time for dealing with transitions & temptations.

Try banishing spells to help overcome harmful magick, hexes, curses & old negativities. The waning phases are most conducive to magick that repels & destroys. The moon in Capricorn is a great time for banishing old fears as well.

Be aware that sadness, depression & fear of failure is common under the Capricorn moon; to the point that it can cause spellwork to falter. Carve a charm into a stone or root for strength & determination to remind yourself of your commitment

when trying to banish & break a bad habit; Capricorn charges
the energy of earth magick.

Capricorn represents structure, stability & groundedness. This
is a great time for centering & grounding rituals. Cooking is
a very grounding exercise, especially when using ingredients
that vibe with this purpose, like sage & black pepper. Though,
botanically a fruit, squash resonates with the element of
earth. Here's a recipe for protective & grounding roast
spaghetti squash:

I. Cut a clean spaghetti squash in half lengthwise. Use a
spoon to scoop out the seeds & ribbing.
2. Drizzle the inside of each half with olive oil, then
sprinkle evenly with salt, crushed sage & black pepper.
3. On a baking sheet, place the two halves facedown with a
sprig of fresh rosemary & a clove of garlic under each
half. Poke holes in the skin of each half using a fork.
4. Roast in the oven for 30-40 minutes at 400°F.
5. Remove from oven & let cool. Then, using a fork, scrape
the squash into noodle-like strands.

Moon water charged under a waning moon is used for grounding,
as well as releasing & letting go, but Capricorn is an
excellent sign if you're looking to harness those grounding
energies for your moon water.

Magick for the Capricorn Waning Crescent Moon

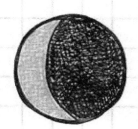

The waning crescent moon in Capricorn occurs from January to July. Therefore, the sun will be under either Capricorn, Aquarius, Pisces, Aries, Taurus, Gemini, Cancer, or Leo. Consider how you can incorporate the energies of both celestial bodies & their signs into your work, and that the waning phases are best for magick that repels, banishes & pushes away what we do not want.

The waning moon is a good time for meditation & introspection, and Capricorn's energies are excellent for making plans, organizing & setting goals. Leo, Aries, Aquarius, Pisces, or Gemini can all influence this energy toward creative pursuits, while practical Taurus & Capricorn would have us plan for our monetary goals or job success.

In fact, Capricorn's serious vibes make it a good time for centering & grounding rituals.

This is also a good time for rituals to overcome negative influences & push ourselves onwards. Use the moon's waning energy to banish what is no longer serving you.

Remember that Capricorn charges the energy of earth magick. This can be employed by first whispering what you wish to banish to a stone or painting a sigil on it that represents what you are banishing. Then, take that stone to a reasonably remote, forested area, like a local park, and throw it as far as you can! Yeet yeet!

The waning crescent phase is also a powerful time for casting bigger spells for breaking & banishing. Separation rituals, cord-cutting & breakup spells are excellent under the cold Capricorn waning moon as well.

Eggshells can be employed to break hexes, something the waning Capricorn moon is perfect for as well. Eggshells & rue are a great combo for this work, as rue is a wonderful herb to use for hex-breaking & the like.

Eggshells also vibe with earthy energy & are powerful symbols of protection. Grind them up with a mortar & pestle into a coarse powder to draw circles of protection before rituals.

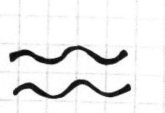

Aquarius Magick

RULING PLANETS: ♄
♅ Uranus & Saturn

SPELLS FOR:
dreaming & divination
creativity & innovation
friendship
connection
freedom

AIR MAGICK: △
When the moon is in an
air sign, like Aquarius,
magick involving
feathers, knots, or your
voice is rather effective.

Air's elemental
direction is east.

The element of
air is associated with
wands or ceremonial
blades.

TAROT:
the Star
king of swords
knight of cups
5,6,7 of swords

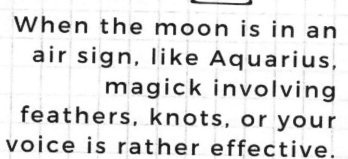

CRYSTALS:
lapis lazuli, aquamarine,
garnet, sapphire, onyx,
turquoise
& amethyst

HERBS:
rosemary, nettles,
fennel, lavender,
burdock, clove,
mint & vervain

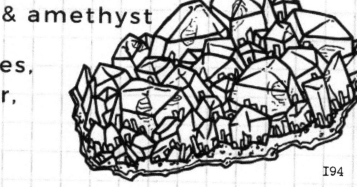

Magick for the Aquarius New Moon

The Aquarius new moon occurs with the sun in Aquarius as well, around the end of January & the beginning of February.

In the Northern Hemisphere, this places us in winter, but the sun is growing in strength & it is the season of Imbolc. In the Southern Hemisphere, it is the opposite time of year. Keep in mind those seasonal vibes when decorating your altar or planning rituals.

When the moon is truly dark in the sky, it is best to refrain from major spellwork. It is a much better time to prepare for the upcoming lunar cycle. Try spellwork that aids in introspection, reflection, recharging, or renewal.

Seek out social events & pass the long winter nights with friends! Aquarius is a sign of friendship & community. Without your coven, the Aquarius moon can leave you feeling alienated. The dual Aquarian energy being channeled makes any group spells especially powerful. Selfish magick can flounder during the Aquarian moon; focus on others & your relationships in your spellwork.

Invite over your fellow witches & host an ingredient swap. Aquarius loves innovation & connection. Or call your clan & smoke cleanse with lavender, yarrow & sage; all of which are powerful under this sign. Do a tarot or rune reading for a friend, or have your coven help you decipher your messages.

The new moon is also when you should set intentions for the upcoming lunar cycle. Aquarius is ruled in part by Uranus, the planet of innovation & originality, and by Saturn, which grants us discipline. Between the two, we have the perfect energy to figure out what you need to manifest your goals, and to get it done!

Have your coven help you set those intentions! Hair braiding is a powerful form of knot magick, which is empowered under airy Aquarius, and you can perform it alone or with your circle. Make a ritual out of it. Braid lengths of ribbon written with your intentions into each other's hair; choose colors that correspond to that intent.

Aquarius brings revelations & big ideas. It's a sign of transformation & looking to the future — perfect for divination or dreamwork. The new moon is an excellent phase for this work as well.

Keeping a dream journal is a perfect way to help keep track of our subconscious, and done routinely will aid in recalling dreams more often & with better detail. Smoking mugwort before bed can encourage dreams as well.

A dream sachet placed under your pillow can also help encourage dreams & remembering them. Use a purple pouch if possible, as it is the color of intuition & psychic energy. It can be stuffed with a multitude of herbs, including lavender, jasmine, chamomile, mugwort, and valerian. Or you can use a cotton ball doused with a few drops of these herbs' essential oils if you prefer. Angelite & moonstone are great gems to include to help you recall your dreams as well. After charging your ingredients with your intent & placing them into the pouch, seal it with a blue cord for communication & truth. Then place it under your pillow to let it do its work!

As an air sign, sometimes Aquarius energies are quite restless, and as an air sign, sometimes a bit chaotic. This can cause spellwork to flounder, but grounding yourself beforehand can help to counteract these fickle energies.

Magick for the Aquarius Waxing Crescent Moon

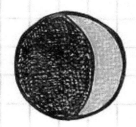

The waxing crescent moon in Aquarius occurs from August to February. This means that the sun can reside in Leo, Virgo, Libra, Scorpio, Sagittarius, Capricorn, Aquarius, or Pisces. Tailor your spells to fit the energies of both celestial bodies — or don't! And simply focus on the moon.

Call your clan for a group ritual. Without your coven, the Aquarius moon can leave you feeling alienated. This can be doubly so with the sun in another social sign like Leo, Libra, or Sagittarius. However, these energies also make group spellwork especially powerful.

It is also a good time to set foundations for future friendships. Use the waxing moon's energy to bring what is outside yourself in. Under an Aquarius moon, we crave connection. It is a sign of friendships & community; burning a bay leaf with the name of a potential friend on it is a simple, but effective way to manifest that goal.

You can also place a tarot card that represents a particular person, or just a type of person, that you want in your life

on your altar for the duration of the waxing cycle to draw
them to you. Just don't forget to put those plans in motion &
reach out to that person too!

Selfish magic falters during the Aquarian moon, so focus on
others in your casting. Lavender is quite useful in spells
for love & bonding; burn it or use it in jar/sachet spell.
Make a magickally charged meal for a friend or relative.
Imbue it with love. Nothing says you care quite like cooking!

Lavender is also great for divination & dreaming spells,
which are in sync with Aquarius' energy. Air signs allow for
curiosity; let it lead the way.

Air magick is potent right now. Work with knot magick, wands,
feathers & your breath to harness the element. Spinning,
weaving, sewing & working with thread, in general, has vast
potential for meditation & magickal works.

Or try cleansing your space with sound or song.

The element of air is a quick-moving element. As an air sign,
Aquarius imparts these elemental energies into spellwork. Use
this energy when you want rapid results.

Magick for the Aquarius First Quarter Moon

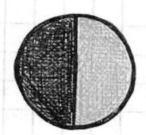

The first quarter moon in Aquarius occurs from August to February, when the sun is under either Leo, Virgo, Libra, Scorpio, Sagittarius, Capricorn, Aquarius, or Pisces.

Consider how you can incorporate the energies of both celestial bodies & their signs into your work. Use the first quarter moon's energy to summon down the creative vibes that the Aquarius moon provides; the sun in Leo, Libra, or Pisces also aids in focusing your creativity.

Burn away roadblocks with some lemongrass incense. Or try using mint in your spell work. It can uplift & empower you when floundering during creative ventures & new projects, and it vibes well with Aquarius. The scent alone is quite powerful; brew mint tea & sip to replenish your energy.

The Aquarius moon can leave you feeling lonely, so call up your coven! After all, Aquarius is a sign of friendship & connection. Host a night of bonding with your brethren.

Try a creative focus; a tye-dye party, some chill coloring,

or even making friendship bracelets. Knot magic is associated with the element of air, and the repetitive knots involved are wonderful for storing magickal energies.

Knot magic allows you to focus and concentrate your energy into the physical realm by creating a physical manifestation of your wants. Different color threads are used for different intentions; the possibilities are endless!

The first quarter moon is great for relationship spells of all sorts, and selfish magic flounders during the Aquarian moon. Keep attitudes sweet in your circle of friends by making sweet jars. The power of the growing moon can be used to attract sweetness into your lives. In a small jar with a tight lid, place a scrap of paper with the recipient's name alongside herbs & crystals for love & prosperity. Rose petals, lavender, amethyst, and rose quartz all vibe well with Aquarius. Finish filling your jar by topping it off with sugar or honey. Then seal it with pink wax & a kiss!

Dreamwork also comes naturally under an Aquarius moon. Before bed bathe in catnip & lavender to leave your body behind; infuse the herbs in hot water, add in some essential oils, or use an herbal bath bomb.

Magick for the Aquarius Waxing Gibbous Moon

The waxing gibbous moon in Aquarius occurs from August to February, meaning the sun can reside in either Leo, Virgo, Libra, Scorpio, Sagittarius, Capricorn, Aquarius, or Pisces.

The waxing phases are perfect for constructive magick of all sorts; spells for magick that pulls our desires towards us. During the gibbous phase, there is little time to harness that energy before the full moon.

Newly cast spells cast should require little turnaround time, as the constructive energies are reaching their peak, and be sure to wrap up any spells that have been simmering over the course of this waxing cycle as well.

The waxing gibbous moon is normally a good phase to recharge our energy. Instead, send those vibes to someone else. Aquarius isn't selfish. It is a sign of friendships & community. So make plans! Plan a ritual with your coven, or just go out with friends. Before having company over, try smoke cleansing with any combination of basil, catnip, or lavender. These herbs all help us feel chill & connected.

Ruled by Uranus, Aquarius is also a sign of transformation. It can help you summon changes in your life. Although you should beware it can be hard to control & oftentimes destructive. Keep the Tower card on your altar to help draw these transformative energies into your life. While the Tower does represent destruction & upheaval, it is always followed by renewal & revelations.

Don't forget to take the time of year into account when decorating your altar or choosing spell ingredients. The seasonal vibes can vary greatly as the waxing Aquarius moon can occur several times from early autumn into late winter.

For example, you can save your Yule greens, like holly & pine, to burn at Imbolc, as these ashes are very powerful — when these plants are burned we can release all sorts of negative energies.

Or you can use pumpkins in the fall to aid in divination work; this type of work is great under Aquarius. Runes, tarot cards, tea leaves, or dreamwork are all viable options. Try burning vervain, mugwort & yarrow, and breathing in the smoke to aid in diving into the unknown.

Magick for the Aquarius Full Moon

The Aquarius full moon occurs when the sun is in Leo. The Leo season spans from July to August, meaning the Aquarius full moon only occurs during one of these two months. If it is July, then the moon is known as the Buck Moon, but in August it is called the Sturgeon Moon.

Both Leo & Aquarius help us connect with our passions & talents, and can help us share them. The combination of these signs can help us figure out where we belong in the world. With the earth caught between the sun & the moon, we have the most powerful celestial energy in the moon's cycle to do so.

Dreaming & divination come naturally at the full moon. Intuition is heightened, and dream interpretation is a great way to guide us towards our place in the world, as well as tarot or rune readings. Aquarius, ruled by Saturn & Uranus, is also a sign of revelations, big ideas & innovation; perfect for this work. Don't forget to set your ritual tools or water to charge in the moonlight too!

For a dream sachet spell, stuff a small bag (purple if you

can manage) with herbs that grant prophetic dreams, like mugwort, peppermint & passionflower, while thyme, chamomile & lavender can aid in protecting against nightmares. Charge under the moonlight before use. The sachet should be placed under a pillow or near a bed to work its magick.

Aquarius is a sign of community & connection; use the full moon to connect & dispel loneliness. Gatherings & group spellwork are especially powerful under an Aquarius moon. It is best to focus on others with your spellwork when the moon is in Aquarius, and especially no selfish magick. So try making your sachet spell for another.

Events can often feel charged or fated under an Aquarius moon. We crave a sense of belonging to something larger, so go out & find your tribe. Host a coven meeting, get involved in your community, or just call up your bestie! Don't get trapped in negative energies.

Before your group ritual harness the element of air, and cleanse your space. Fragrances & feathers are very in tune with this element. Use a feather duster to wipe stale energy off your shelves. Afterward, use scents like rosemary, lavender, or mugwort in a diffuser, or by smoke cleansing.

You can also use sound to cleanse with the element of air; bells, chimes, instruments & even voices can work. Witch's bells are a beautiful tool representative of air. Various lengths of ribbon or cord are used to attach bells, charms, and protective herbs to a metal or wooden ring. Hang them on knobs or ring them while walking out a circle.

Bells are also sometimes used in fertility spells, as the bell's body represents the womb, and the bell's clapper represents a phallus. With the sun in passionate Leo, it can be a good time for a fertility ritual that involves alone time with your partner!

As an air sign, air magick is potent under Aquarius! Just be careful as the element also brings a chaotic nature with it, which can get in the way of your magick.

Onions & garlic can bring grounding energy to airy Aquarius. Onions also absorb negative energy, and garlic has protective properties. Braiding your onions, shallots, or garlic is not only the perfect way to store them, but also potent knot magick, which channels Aquarius' elemental energy. They are easy to braid too!

Starting with 3 long lengths of twine knotted at one end, gently braid the necks of your garlic or onions using a French braid method. Start with your longest greens, adding another into each twist as you go. As you braid, be sure to focus on your intention. Tie off the end with twine, or tie remaining greens into a loop. Hang as a charm in your kitchen to continue to keep you grounded and to ward away bad energy.

Magick for the Aquarius Waning Gibbous Moon

The waning gibbous moon in Aquarius can occur from February to August. This means that the sun will be in either Aquarius, Pisces, Aries, Taurus, Gemini, Cancer, Leo, or Virgo. Spellwork can use the energies of both these signs, but the waning phases are best for magick that repels, banishes & destroys things, pushing away what we do not want.

The Aquarius waning gibbous moon can occur multiple times throughout the year; mainly in early spring & summer. This is a perfect time to venture outdoors to gather materials or perform a ritual.

You can use the entire waning cycle to work some big magick — remember intricate spellwork will be more easily accomplished with the sun in Virgo!

However, for the few days after the full moon, energies can feel sapped & slow as the moon recedes, making it a good time for introspection. If you keep a dream journal, it is a good time to sit down and assess it! Review what you have recorded and look for patterns & premonitions.

Aquarius is also a sign of revelations & transformation. Divination & dreamwork work well under this sign. But during the waning moon, look to the past and seek out introspection rather than divine the future.

Aquarius is a social sign; banish drama, any feelings of jealousy & bad vibes between people. This is especially potent spellwork if the sun is also in a social sign, like Cancer, Leo, or Aquarius. Burn basil, lavender & rosemary to be rid of resentments. If you can't have smoke where you live or if you are sensitive to it, try using essential oils & moon water in a diffuser!

Craving a sense of belonging to something larger? Dispel loneliness; gatherings & group spellwork work well under an Aquarius moon. Call your clan and dance under the moon's waning light. Make a playlist just for the occasion.

Air magick is also potent right now; utilize knots & your voice in your rituals. Knots in a piece of string are a great tool for binding & banishing.

Take a length of black cord and speak aloud what you are using it to 'tie up'. Then proceed to loop your first knot, stating your intent aloud as the knot shrinks. Repeat this five more times for a total of six knots, speaking your intent each time as you slowly pull the knot together. Store in a safe place where it can be put out of mind.

Magick for the Aquarius Last Quarter Moon

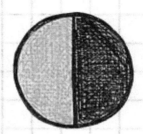

The last quarter moon in Aquarius occurs from February to August when the sun is under either Aquarius, Pisces, Aries, Taurus, Gemini, Cancer, Leo, or Virgo. The energies of both those signs should be considered in spellwork as well.

For example, the energies of an Aquarian moon are quite social. Group rituals & spellwork are especially powerful if both the sun & moon are in Aquarius. But another social sign, like Leo or Gemini, will vibe well with this too.

The waning phases are most conducive to magick that repels or destroys. These energies can be harnessed to break up relationships or resolve disputes. For a firm end to a relationship, use a cord-cutting ritual. This can be with a friend, lover, a job, or even an unhealthy habit — and the last quarter moon is excellent for breaking bad habits!

Simply tie your string — use something natural like hemp or cotton, so the fumes are not toxic — around two black candles, firmly planted on a plate or candle holder, and then light the candles.

As the candle burns down, it will soon reach the strings and sever the tie between the two people. Be sure to visualize that energetic cord severing & to state your intentions as you work. And of course, cleanse your space before you work!

You can also use Aquarius' airy elemental energy in your banishing spells. Bubbles or dandelion seeds work well for this. Just visualize your intention, take a deep breath, and blow! Let the wind carry what you need out of your life for good. Make sure to do this on a breezy day!

The last quarter moon is also a particularly good time for rest & reflection. And Aquarius makes meditation easier!

During the waning moon, it is better to look towards the past rather than the future, but Aquarius's energies still aid in divination & dreamwork. This is especially true if the sun is in either Gemini, Cancer, or Pisces.

Magick for the Aquarius Waning Crescent Moon

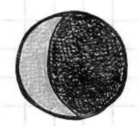

The waning crescent moon in Aquarius can occur from February to August. This means that the sun will be in either Aquarius, Pisces, Aries, Taurus, Gemini, Cancer, Leo, or Virgo. Your spellwork can work with the energies of both signs, as well as seasonal energies.

Aquarius is a rebel, a sign that shuns the status quo. These creative, non-conforming energies pair well with dispelling blocks in our creative ventures. The sun in either Pisces, Leo, or Gemini vibes well with this too. Burning nettles, lemongrass & rosemary banishes those obstacles, while mint tea will help replenish your energy when floundering during creative ventures & new projects.

The waning crescent is an extremely powerful time for casting out anything you no longer want in your life, and banishing spells are a great way to do so. This close to the dark moon is when these energies are at their strongest. Release energies that aren't serving you.

Cast a spell to release anger & cool tempers. In a small jar, mix moon water, mint oil, and aloe vera gel. Then, write the reason for anger on a slip of paper & burn it using a black candle. As the candle burns, dip your finger in the jar and draw a circle counterclockwise over your heart while breathing out. Feel your heart cooling. Let that anger go!

Events can often feel charged or fated under an Aquarius moon. Connect with someone else for a tarot reading. Aquarius celebrates the gathering of many — and all their unique approaches to life!

Ritual gatherings & group spellwork are especially powerful under this social sign. But remember to look to the past for answers during the waning phases, not the future. Aquarius is all about the collective, and under the waning moon, we can look back at ourselves and consider what we need to let go of to be a better friend, partner, roommate, etc.

Harness the element of air & try singing or chanting a spell. This can be amplified with many voices; air signs are symbolic of connection. If singing isn't your thing, make noise in another way. Have everyone bring a bell instead and form a circle to ring them in tandem; this energy can be focused into a powerful banishing or cleansing ritual.

Pisces Magick

RULING PLANETS:

 Neptune & Jupiter ♃

SPELLS FOR:

dreaming & divination
beauty & the arts
healing
cleansing

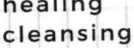

WATER MAGICK:

When the moon resides under a water sign, like Pisces, magick involving water is particularly effective; especially natural water like the ocean or rain.

Water's elemental direction is west.

The element of water is also associated with cauldrons or chalices.

TAROT:

the Moon
queen of wands
knight of cups
8, 9, 10 of cups

HERBS:

sage,
yarrow,
nettles,
lavender, borage,
basil, dandelion
& passionflower,

CRYSTALS:

moonstone,
amethyst,
aquamarine,
sapphire
& pearl

Magick for the Pisces New Moon

The new moon in Pisces occurs with the sun also in Pisces, at the end of February & the beginning of March.

As the last sign of the zodiac, Pisces is a bridge between this life & the next. Divination & psychic work come naturally during this time of rebirth. Spiritual Pisces is one of the best signs for it. Reflect and tune into something greater than yourself.

Beginning a dream journal or mood tracker is perfect under intuitive Pisces. Use it the entire lunar cycle, then compare it to the lunar calendar to see if there are any correlations!

You can also tap into Pisces's dreamy energy with a tarot or rune reading. Burn mugwort & yarrow to aid in diving into the unknown. Or try bathing in mugwort, chamomile & lavender to reconnect with the power of the cosmic mother.

Recharging & resting near water vibes with Pisces's elemental energy. Any spells involving water are charged under Pisces &

water is the element most in tune with the moon. You can tap also into those energies by making moon water. Leave it out to charge in the moonless night to imbue the water with energies for fresh starts, intention setting, and cleansing. Seawater has fantastic cleansing properties, which vibe with the new moon's energies as well. Use it in a ritual bath or to wipe down your altar or ritual tools.

Imbued with the essence of the sea, seashells cleanse objects they are placed near, and they are great tools to use for water elemental magick as well.

Differently shaped shells can hold different meanings, and a set of similar shells can be used to make a set of runes that vibe with the element of water.

Many are also natural vessels, perfect for holding moon water or, when properly cleaned, ritual beverages like wine. They are also helpful in drawing down the moon, but this ritual is better performed during a full moon rather than the new moon.

Remember, when the moon is truly dark in the sky, it is best to refrain from major spellwork. It is better to prepare & plan for the upcoming lunar cycle, but cleansings & purification are in tune with Pisces as well as the new moon.

After tidying up, fill a saucepan, kettle, or cauldron with moon water & let simmer. Add dried fruit & herbs to create an aromatic aura in your home. Cinnamon, honey, and clove encourage pleasant attitudes, while citrus can clear negativity & brighten your home!

Pisces is also a sign of compassion, forgiveness, deep emotions, & unconditional love. You can use this energy to help others. It is, however, easy to lose yourself in these

energies. Be sure to ground yourself first, so you don't
drain your own resources too much.

In fact, the Pisces moon is an excellent time to pamper
yourself with a beauty or glamour spell. Lavender responds
very well under Pisces as well, and it is excellent for this
type of spellwork. Try a lavender honey hair mask to bestow
yourself with confidence & shiny hair:

- 3 tablespoons of honey
- 3 tablespoons olive oil
- 10 drops of lavender essential oil

1. Heat honey & olive oil in the microwave. It should be
   warm, but not hot!
2. Add essential oils & mix.
3. Massage into hair, starting at the ends. Use enough to
   drench hair, then wrap in a towel.
4. Leave on for 30+ minutes. Super dry hair may absorb quite
   a bit, and any leftovers can be applied as it absorbs.
5. Wash hair normally afterward.

Magick for the Pisces Waxing Crescent Moon

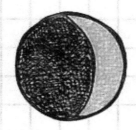

The waxing crescent moon in Pisces can occur from September to March. This means the sun can reside under either Virgo, Libra, Scorpio, Sagittarius, Capricorn, Aquarius, Pisces, or Aries. Use the energies of both these signs to fuel your spellwork!

For example, Libra & Pisces make the perfect pairing for a glamour or beauty spell — try painting a sigil directly on your skin with your concealer before blending!

Pisces is a sign of compassion & unconditional love. Use this energy to heal yourself or help others. Volunteer or take time to help a loved one out. Use the waxing moon's pull to conjure positive energies to bring about positive change.

Food is always a powerful pull to get together, and if you are looking to do something seasonal, soup fits perfectly into the colder months of the year. Encourage community in your coven or friend group by making a 'group soup' by asking each person to bring an ingredient. When you gather together & cook, stir the pot clockwise to invite positivity & good health into your circle.

Water aids us in expressing our emotions & drawing out our feelings; maybe this is why creativity thrives under Pisces. Harness those energies; add moon water to your watercolors to charge them while painting. Use those watercolors to paint sigils or write out what you wish to manifest. Or use the waxing moon's energy to commit to writing or learning a new song. The moon in Pisces truly has crazy creative energy to help you along, as this sign is in part ruled by Neptune, the planet of dreams & imagination.

Moonstone, exceptionally in tune with Pisces, should be charged under the waxing moon when the moon's energies are restorative & growing in power. The full moon can be too powerful for this gem.

Spiritual Pisces is also one of the best signs for divination, dreamwork & psychic work. But it is a very bad sign for protection spells.

Be cautious when working under a Pisces moon, as exhaustion & absent-mindedness can cause your spellwork to flounder!

Magick for the Pisces First Quarter Moon

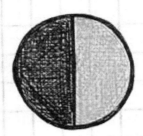

The first quarter moon in Pisces occurs from September to March, which means that the sun can be in either Virgo, Libra, Scorpio, Sagittarius, Capricorn, Aquarius, Pisces, or Aries. Your spellwork can suit both signs, of course.

Libra & Pisces vibe well with spells for beauty & creativity, while Aquarius or Scorpio work better with spellwork for dreams or divining.

Pisces in particular lets us slip away from the physical world; intuition is especially heightened & divination comes naturally. So read your runes, break out your pendulum, or do a tarot spread! Whatever method works best for you!

Try surrounding yourself with moonstones & amethysts, as they can boost your intuition! Burning mugwort & yarrow aid in tapping into spiritual energies too!

To summon dreams, bathe in chamomile, catnip & lavender before bed. Or stuff a sachet instead, but remember spells involving the element of water are charged under Pisces. A few tea bags — as easy as the ones from the grocery store — make a simple ritual bath. Look for blends containing herbs of your choice. There are many relaxing blends with potent magickal herbs like lavender & chamomile. Just toss a few under the hot, running water before you get it!

Tea leaves are also a marvelous means of divination. Simply spoon loose leaf tea directly into a cup of hot water, then drink until the final dregs are left. There should be just enough to swirl around the bottom. Do so three times, counterclockwise, with your cup in your left hand. Then turn the cup upside down to drain for a moment before reading.

You can look for patterns, shapes, signs & symbols in the dregs, but there are also teacups that are marked for especially for divination.

Pisces wants us to be the light in the darkness of the world, but it can be easy to drown in the darkness. During a Pisces moon, it is easy to get lost in self-pity or be upset easily. Don't get lost in bad vibes! They can work negatively with your spells!

Call down energy for positive change; or better yet, go out and volunteer. Make the world better. Pisces calls for us to be charitable & compassionate.

Magick for the Pisces Waxing Gibbous Moon

The waxing gibbous moon in Pisces occurs from September to March. This means that at this time the sun can be in either Virgo, Libra, Scorpio, Sagittarius, Capricorn, Aquarius, Pisces, or Aries.

The waxing gibbous moon is the last stage before the full moon & when we must trust that the intentions we set will come to fruition. During this phase, we can take the last steps we need to reach our goals & manifest our intentions. With the moon under Pisces, this pertains especially to our creative ventures!

Water rituals are powerful under a Pisces moon, and doubly so if the sun also sits under a water sign. Unfortunately, not all of us have the tub of our dreams to soak in! However, never underestimate the power of a homemade, aromatic body wash! Make & bless your own ritual body wash for a more meditative shower:

- ½ cup shea butter
- 2 tablespoons olive or jojoba oil

- 2 tablespoons vegetable glycerin
- I0-20 drops of essential oils
- I cup liquid castile soap

I. Melt the shea butter in a double boiler, then slowly fold in the rest of the ingredients with a spatula. If you go too quickly, there will be bubbles!
2. Let cool & pour your body wash into a jar using a funnel.

Under the waxing moon, use your body wash. Begin at your toes & work your way up to your head to invite good energy in with the strength of the growing moon.

Pisces can leave you feeling world-weary, so boost your energy with mint & lemongrass tea. The energy sap that Pisces brings can affect spellwork! Be self-indulgent & use the moon's energy to restore your spirit. Pisces is a sign of compassion, forgiveness, deep emotions & unconditional love. Use this energy to heal yourself.

The Pisces moon is a bad time for protection spells, but Pisces energizes beauty & glamour spells. Spells involving water are also potent under Pisces; use moon water to wash your face & call down clear skin.

Spiritual Pisces is also one of the best signs for divination & dreamwork. As the last sign of the zodiac, Pisces is a bridge between this life & the next. Our intuition is very heightened!

Seasonal energies & the time of day can also be considered when casting.

Magick for the Pisces Full Moon

The full moon in Pisces occurs with the sun in Virgo. As the Virgo season spans from August to September, this means the Pisces full moon only occurs during these two months. If it is August the moon is known as the Sturgeon Moon, but in September it is called the Harvest Moon.

The combination of Pisces & Virgo makes this an excellent time for cleansings. Use sound or smoke, or cleanse your space with an herbal infusion of mint — brew it like tea! Then, dip a rag in the liquid & dust. Remember to state your intentions to cleanse bad energy clearly as you work!

White vinegar can also be charged under the full moon's light and used to clean your home! Mix it with mop water & essential oils, or run it through your dishwater or washing machine to cleanse their energies.

Spellwork with water is potent under Pisces & especially bath magick. Bless water in the light of the full moon or leave it to charge. Collect rainwater if you can!

Or simply take a bath with an herbal bath bomb! Here's how to make them at home:

- 4 I/2 cups of baking soda
- I/2 cups Epsom salts
- 2 cups of cornstarch
- 2 cups citric acid
- I/2 cups fresh, chopped herbs
- I-3 tsp of water
- 6 tsp coconut oil
- 20ish drops of essential oils
- I0 drops of natural dye (optional)

I. First, mix the dry ingredients thoroughly. In a separate dish, mix the wet ingredients. Use a whisk or a mixer for this; the oils and water take some work to blend together.
2. Then, slowly you add the wet mix to the dry. This must be done slowly, so the dry ingredients don't activate. Otherwise, you end up with a not-so-fizzy bath bomb. Try applying the water with a spray bottle if you are struggling! The mixture should feel like damp sand and clump when pressed together.
3. Then press the mix into your mold, let it sit for 30 seconds, and tap out. Repeat.
4. Let dry overnight before you use. Store in an airtight container. This will make about a dozen depending on the mold size.

For a spiritually cleansing bath, use rosemary & sage to delve into the unknown use mugwort, lavender & catnip.

Pisces exudes mysticism & spirituality. Divination, dreamwork & psychic work come naturally under Pisces & especially during the full moon. It's easy to leave our bodies behind in

this time of rebirth. Emotions & intuition are all naturally
heightened at this time.

We can work with this heightened intuition further by drawing
down the moon & calling on her to fill us with her light.
Traditionally done outside — this is a great time of year for
it — this ritual is performed, arms raised, with a chant to
the moon to fill us with her energy. It can induce a trance-
state, and leave us with a feeling of clarity afterwards.

Under the sensitive Pisces moon, spells for music & art also
thrive. Imagination & fantasy can run wild under the Pisces
moon. Use that creative force! Plan on working on your
creative pursuits — dance, paint, write!

Pisces is also a sign of immense empathy. Don't let yourself
be swallowed up by the sufferings in the world. Turn off the
news or take a break from social media if you need to! It
takes courage to choose your own peace sometimes!

Magick for the Pisces Waning Gibbous Moon

The waning gibbous moon in Pisces occurs from March to September, meaning the sun will reside in either Pisces, Aries, Taurus, Gemini, Cancer, Leo, Virgo, or Libra. Take the energies of both signs into account as you work, or focus on the moon alone!

Keep in mind that for a few days after the full moon, your energy can feel sapped & slow as the moon recedes, especially when the moon is in Pisces. Lack of energy is a good reason to hold off on casting anything. It can cause a spell to not work out how we want it to. This is especially true under a Pisces moon. So rest up & do what you can, when you can!

If you do have the energy, you can use the waning moon's destructive energy to banish blocks in creative energy; let whatever is stifling your creative spirit wane with the moon. Pisces energizes any spells empowering the arts, including music, dance & poetry.

Intense emotions can also be banished by belting out an appropriate song; crank up the volume & let loose.

Or try cleansing your energy, your home & your creative tools by smoke cleansing with sage & other herbs. Bathe everything in smoke — just be careful not to set off any smoke alarms!

Pisces also vibes strongly with any natural bodies of water, and the waning Pisces moon can occur multiple times from spring into fall. This means there are multiple opportunities to make a trip to a lake, a river, or the seaside.

These places are power locations, spiritually & physically, to collect magickal ingredients, including sand, stones, shells, water & more. Just remember to be respectful of nature's power, and to never swim alone!

Pisces' watery elemental energies can be used for banishing spells under the waning moon as well. Go to a local stream, creek, or river, find a nearby leaf. Write upon it, or whisper to it, what you need carried out of your life. Then, place it in the water & send it on its way.

Divination & dreamwork also come naturally under super spiritual Pisces, but during the waning moon, it is best to look to the past for answers rather than trying to decipher what the future will bring.

Magick for the Pisces Last Quarter Moon

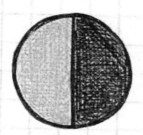

The last quarter moon in Pisces occurs from March to September, meaning it can fall when the sun is in either Pisces, Aries, Taurus, Gemini, Cancer, Leo, Virgo, or Libra. The waning moon occurs from the moment the moon begins to fade from the full phase until it disappears once more.

The last quarter moon is the halfway point between them and is most conducive to magick that repels, banishes, or destroys. Remember to take both the sun & the moon's signs into account when casting.

Pisces energizes spells for music & the arts — use the waning moons to banish blocks in creativity. This works especially well when the sun is in Gemini, Leo, Libra, or Pisces.

Or try a facemask of the fresh aloe vera gel to illuminate your skin — Pisces & Libra are great signs for beauty spells. The gel is a natural moisturizer for the skin and can also help calm acne and redness. Let the gel dry and bask in the waning moonlight to banish blemishes.

The healing energies of the Pisces moon are amplified with the sun in Aries, Gemini, or Virgo; so use the waning moon's energy to banish illness as well. Imbue a tincture of mugwort, chickweed, cover, and stinging nettles with those energies. Fill a sealable jar with a combination of these herbs. Then, cover the leaves with apple cider vinegar & let it sit in a dark place for 2-4 weeks. Shake every day. This elixir wards off anemia & brittle bones. It makes an excellent vinaigrette and can be eaten on salads or it can be taken by the tablespoon as a tonic.

The energies of the Pisces waning moon can also be used to banish bad dreams. Pisces is one of the best signs for dreamwork & divination; intuition can be very heightened. This makes it a good time to review any dream journals, mood trackers, or diaries you keep. Compare them to a lunar calendar to see if the moon has any correlation to your mood or the power of your dreams.

Scry with pre-charged moon water — perfectly in sync with Pisces' elemental energies, do a tarot reading, or cast some runes. And using a book, like a dictionary, for divination vibes with the intellectual nature of air signs like Aquarius. With the waning moon, it is best to look towards the past for answers.

It is also an excellent time to reflect, as Pisces is a sign of deep emotions & empathy.

Magick for the Pisces Waning Crescent Moon

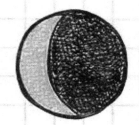

The waning crescent moon in Pisces occurs from March to September. This means the sun is in either Pisces, Aries, Taurus, Gemini, Cancer, Leo, Virgo, or Libra.

Don't forget to take the time of year into account when making offerings, decorating your altar, or choosing spell ingredients. The waning Pisces moon can occur multiple times from early spring into fall, meaning there is a plethora of fresh flowers & herbs available.

The Pisces waning crescent is a powerful time to banish bad energy & cleanse the home. The energies are especially cleansing if the sun happens to be in Cancer, Virgo, or Pisces as well. Use this energy to wash your bedsheets with a few drops of lavender & chamomile essential oils, which can help banish sleep disturbances too. Or smoke cleanse with lavender & sage; they both sync well with Pisces' energy.

The waning phases are most in sync with spells that repel or banish. The waning crescent is a powerful time for casting bigger banishing & casting out anything you no longer want in your life. Release energies that aren't serving you and push away anything that is holding you back. This close to the dark moon is when these energies are at their strongest.

Beauty spells are potent under Pisces; spells to banish poor self-confidence and bad impressions. Write down what you wish gone from your life gently on toilet paper & then flush it down the toilet. If the paper tears, it could mean you aren't meant to leave it behind just yet! Water magick is powerful under gentle Pisces, and the waning moon's energy is perfect for banishing!

Reflect & tune into something greater than yourself; try journaling under the waning moonlight. Pisces is a great sign for journaling! The watery sign aids us in expressing emotion & drawing out our feelings.

Remember your rituals & spellwork can be affected by Pisces's energies negatively too; they can leave us feeling tired & distracted.

REFERENCES

Planetary Spells & Rituals: Practicing Dark & Light Magick Aligned with the Cosmic Bodies by Raven Digitalis

Moon Spells for Beginners: A Guide to Moon Magic, Lunar Phases, and Essential Spells & Rituals by Michael Herkes

Magickal Astrology: Use the Power of the Planets to Create an Enchanted Life by Skye Alexander

The Good Witch's Guide: A Modern-Day Wiccapedia of Magickal Ingredients & Spells by Shawn Robbins & Charity Bedell

New World Witchery: A Trove of North American Folk Magic by Cory Thomas Hutcheson

The Moon Book: Lunar Magic to Change Your Life by Sarah Faith Gottesdiener

Sabbats: A Witch's Approach to Living the Old Ways by Edain McCoy

Earth, Air, Fire & Water by Scott Cunningham

Encyclopedia of Magickal Herbs by Scott Cunningham

Green Witchcraft: A Practical Guide to Discovering the Magic of Plants, Herbs, Crystals & Beyond by Paige Vanderbeck

ABOUT THE AUTHORS

Quinn is an artist, witch, and fanatical gardener who barely attended college at Tyler School of Art. Her roots are in Philadelphia, but she currently resides in the rural South. Her published works include various articles & short stories in witchy zines & magazines. This is her debut book. Check out her Instagram to see what she's been working on!

With an open and avid mind, Morgan is an artist, author, witch, and generally multi-faceted Gemini, filling her life with friends, family, gardens, festivals, and a small collection of exceptionally perfect pets. With much of her roots in the swampy, rural south, she also attended the Savannah College of Art and Design and received a bachelor of fine arts degree. Many years later, she finally decided to use it. Keep up with her on Instagram!

WWW.THEMOONMANUAL.COM

Ⓟ @THEMOONMANUAL

Ⓞ @THEMOONMANUAL

Lightning Source UK Ltd.
Milton Keynes UK
UKHW052032070223
416603UK00008B/76

9 798985 593907